PURCHASE POWER RETIREMENT FORMULA (PPRF):

THE SECRET STRATEGY FOR ACHIEVING THE RETIREMENT OF YOUR DREAMS...ON ANY BUDGET

Idris Manley

Founder and CEO of Retirocracy

DEDICATION

To my father, Harold Manley (1932 – 2017), blessed with talents and gifts beyond measure. Thank you for inspiring me early in life to be fearless in my pursuit of happiness.

To Miles, Ellington, Sydney, Blair, and Langston. You give me life, inspiration, and hope for a better future. I love you to pieces.

With special gratitude to Dorothy Manley, the best mother I could ever imagine. Your love, encouragement, and determination have helped make me into the person I am today.

Why Read This Book?

Ask yourself these questions:

- Are you NOT on track for achieving your retirement savings goal?
- Will your retirement standard of living be worse than your pre-retirement lifestyle?
- Is the thought of retiring stressful?
- If money wasn't an issue, would that change how you prepared for or thought about retirement?
- If you could retire early, would you?
- Should retirement be the most interesting and exciting chapter of your life?
- Should your retirement experience reflect your values, interests and passions?
- Do you have the right to experience the retirement of your dreams?

If you answered yes to even one of these questions, this book is for you.

DISCLAIMER

The content here contains personal opinions of the author regarding financial matters. It is for educational purposes only. The publisher and author do not imply or intend any guarantee of accuracy. The information here is not necessarily suitable for every individual: Use it at your own risk. No guarantees are made that you will achieve results similar to those described here, or any specific results whatsoever from using the concepts and approaches discussed. No guarantees are implied or expressed. Though reasonable effort has been taken to make this material as useful as possible, there may be typographical mistakes or errors in the content. Neither the author nor the publisher is engaged in rendering professional services including but not limited to accounting, tax, legal, or investment planning. This information is not intended as a substitute for such professional services. If specific advice is needed or appropriate, the reader should seek out and engage a licensed professional. The author and publisher specifically disclaim any liability, loss or risk taken by readers who directly or indirectly act on this information. You are solely responsible for your own decisions and actions, and their results.

Table of Contents

Author's Preface

Writing this book was a true labor of love. I sought to inspire all who may have fallen short of their savings goals yet still desire to experience the most life has to offer during retirement. This book is for all who have done everything they thought was necessary for a successful retirement, including working their butts off for 20-40+ years of their lives, only to discover that the retirement lifestyle they envisioned may not exist.

Every American citizen has the right and ability to maintain and even improve his or her lifestyle after retirement. I will help you set even higher expectations for your retirement future and encourage you to embrace the idea that your lifestyle should continue to improve, not decline, with age. At the end of the day, your best, most exciting, fulfilling years are not behind you, but ahead of you, waiting to be fully unleashed once you retire.

Over the course of this book, I will help you set a new vision for what life after the rat race should look like. I will also help you better understand why, if you play it safe by society's rules, you may unknowingly sabotage your future retirement lifestyle.

There are countless "financial experts" promoting retirement strategies focused on helping you make more money, save more money and invest better. While important, those strategies are not the focus of this book. My goal is to help you set a new course for achieving your dream retirement by introducing you to a growing movement of people who are determined not to allow their retirement future to be defined just by how much they have saved. These individuals are taking control of their retirement future by leveraging the proven benefits – of a little-understood concept – known as the purchase power principle. I invite you to join this movement of people!

If you are struggling to get your financial retirement plan on track, this book offers you a realistic blueprint for success. You may not realize it, but as future retirees we are at war with institutions that have little regard for our retirement outlook. They are the politicians who continue to make it harder for us to receive our rightful social security income by increasing the retirement age threshold; they are corporations that refuse to support pensions yet embrace retirement vehicles, such as 401(k)s, that transfer the financial management risk to you and me; they are the mega-rich on Wall Street who apply highly sophisticated strategies to get even richer off the backs of Main Street investors.

Many retirees have found retirement to be a disappointing experience. In fact, according to a survey by Nationwide Retirement Institute of adults age 50 or older, 28 percent of recent retirees say life is worse in retirement[1]. But it doesn't have to be that way.

Merrill Lynch and Agewave conducted a joint survey in 2016 about our grasp of the realities of retirement.[2] Over 80 percent of respondents didn't know how much money they'd need in retirement – not too surprising since there are so many factors that impact how much will be needed. Yet retirement is not all about money. According to the survey responses, 95 percent of retirees say they prefer *experiences over things* for their leisure time in retirement. They seek to create better health and less stress for themselves.

Rather than a winding-down period, many want retirement to be a time for new experiences, improved health and increased relaxation. Why not have this yourself?

Through these pages, my hope is to sharpen your vision of the type of retirement you can have. I want this for myself and I want it for all of you who have worked hard and contributed to society and to your families and friends. Nothing *stops* at retirement except punching the time clock. Many new experiences can *begin* on your first day of retirement and continue for years to come.

Retirement may seem a far-off time of your life. Or

you may not have a clear vision of how those years might unfold, what you will be able to do and experience, and just how retirement will play out for you. In other words, the reality of retirement often doesn't sink in until it starts.

The forces and challenges faced by everyday Americans can be overwhelming and even depressing. But there's hope! I encourage you to learn how the Purchase Power Retirement Formula has knowingly and unknowingly transformed the lives of countless Americans, and can transform your retirement lifestyle too.

In Part 1 of this book, I walk you through how we have traditionally been able – or not – to fund our retirement years. Then we'll see why so many of us have obstacles not only in thinking about retirement but in having sufficient funds for it. In Part 2, I take you through a simple and perhaps new process for creating an exceptional lifestyle and a time of joyful experiences in the many, many retirement years awaiting you.

On the next page, The Retirement Manifesto describes the retirement lifestyle that you can have for yourself. Read on to learn how you can experience joy and excitement in your retirement years.

— IDRIS MANLEY

THE RETIREMENT MANIFESTO

We believe all Americans have the right to:

- Experience freedom from financial worry during retirement
- Be flexible and do what they want, when they want
- Make up for lost time with family, friends and acquaintances
- Retire on time or even early, if desired
- Relax and enjoy the stillness of life
- Grow, learn and challenge themselves
- Reinvent themselves and build a better self
- Make a difference
- Go along for the ride and take each day as it comes
- Fall in love with themselves and the world around them ... again
- Be excited about the future and what it will bring
- Give back and help others in need
- Live a lifestyle and quality of life dictated by more than just a savings account

PART 1

Our Retirement Problem...and How It Could Impact You

If you conduct a random survey of 10 people and ask them, "What does retirement mean to you?" you will get 10 different answers. Some hope to travel around the country in an RV; others hope for the stability to lead a relaxing life of poker with friends, growing a garden, and sipping coffee on the front porch; still others worry about having to go to work in a retail store when they're 70. While the answers vary widely, nearly everyone is worried about it.

Today, every worker expects to retire someday, but the concept of retirement did not always exist. Back in 1880, no one retired. If you were drawing breath, you worked.

Life expectancy throughout the 19th century was around 40 years, contrary to our 21st-century expectations of living until at least age 80.

Why 1880? Because the following year is when the concept of "retirement" from the world of work was created. A socialist movement in Europe created a lot of pressure on the governments to go beyond the then-current employer-favorable legislation and do something for workers. In 1881, Otto von Bismarck, who was minister president of Prussia, presented a groundbreaking (and some might have said highly disruptive) idea to the Reichstag. He asked the equivalent of our U.S. Congress to enact government-run financial support for older members of society. In other words – he was asking for a "retirement funding" for the laborers of the day, collectible from age 70.

Turns out that von Bismarck wasn't overreaching. He wasn't asking for too much – not when we consider that the number of people living until age 70 was miniscule at the time. It was a small price to pay to get the labor movement off his back!

So, what has been the retirement support situation since then? You might think it's gotten even better for retired workers. Maybe. Maybe not. In this section, I will show you where we've been since von Bismarck convinced the Reichstag to make that small compromise ... and how far we've come.[3]

CHAPTER 1

THEY DON'T CARE IF YOU EVER RETIRE

Speak with almost any financial advisor about how to retire successfully, and inevitably the retirement strategy will be reduced to encouraging you to accomplish one or more of the following objectives:

1. Increase your income
2. Decrease your expenses
3. Increase returns (profits) on your investments

In my experience, these same advisors never tell you HOW to achieve any of these supposedly "clear" goals!

As you begin to plan for retirement, these financial experts oftentimes insist that you meet *age-specific* savings goals like on the following chart:

RETIREMENT SAVINGS TARGETS BY AGE							
Annual Salary / Target by Age	$50K	$75K	$100K	$150K	$200K	$250K	$300K
35	$15K(.3x)	$90K(1x)	$150K(2x)	$315K(2x)	$520K(3x)	$750K(3x)	$960K(3.2x)
40	$40K(.8x)	$143K(2x)	$230K(2x)	$465K(3x)	$740K(4x)	$1M(4x)	$1.3M(4x)
45	$75K(2x)	$210K(3x)	$330K(3x)	$480K(3x)	$980K(5x)	$1.4M(5x)	$1.7M(6x)
50	$120K(2x)	$293K(4x)	$450K(5x)	$840K(6x)	$1.3M(6x)	$1.8M(7x)	$2.2M(7x)
55	$170K(3x)	$390K(5x)	$590K(6x)	$1M(7x)	$1.6M(8x)	$2.3M(9x)	$2.8M(9x)
60	$225K(5x)	$510K(7x)	$750K(8x)	$1.4M(9x)	$2M(10x)	$2.8M(11x)	$3.5M(12x)
65	$305K(6x)	$660K(9x)	$980K(10x)	$1.8M(12x)	$2.7M(13x)	$3.6M(14x)	$4.4M(15x)

Note: Target savings goal and savings multiple based on present salary, by age.

The top of the chart shows your present annual income, the left column shows your age. The intersections show how much total cash you "should" have saved by that time. The value in the brackets is the multiple of your present salary. The idea is to save the cash in a retirement plan or long-term savings/investment account. Thus, by age 35, assuming you have worked since age 20 or so, you'll have saved $15,000 for retirement, or .3 times your salary if you are earning $50,000 per year. By age 50, you'll have saved $840,000 or six times your salary if you have been earning $150,000 per year, and so on.

The problem with this approach is that before the age of 35 or 40, most of us just aren't ready or in a position to begin saving this aggressively toward retirement. And because we don't, often we are already caught behind the eight ball on saving.

Also confusing the issue, experts may vary on exactly how much you should save at different age milestones. What they do agree on is the need to achieve specific savings targets by age. And why wouldn't they recommend such an approach? This practical strategy makes a lot of sense. Achieving specific savings targets every five years keeps you on a predictable track for having a nice, plump nest egg of cash for retirement.

We are told that our Dream Retirement is at the intersection of making more money, saving more money, and increasing the return/profitability of our investments (or ROI, often achieved through the effect of compounding).

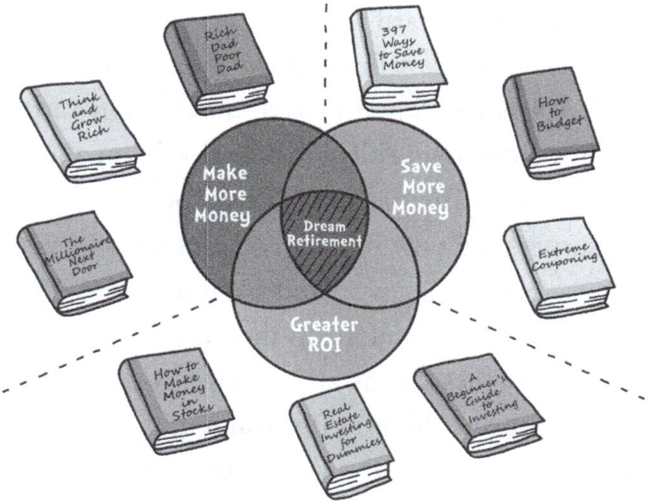

You have probably read your fair share of books and articles to help improve your own proficiency in these areas. I certainly have. My personal library is filled with countless self-help books such as *Rich Dad Poor Dad* by Robert Kiyosaki, *The Millionaire Next Door* by Thomas J. Stanley, *Think and Grow Rich* by Napoleon Hill and numerous books on real estate and stock market investing. There are also all those magazines: *Money* magazine, *Fortune* and so on. For me, it was mandatory to read these books and learn from experts willing to teach me how to maximize my net worth and retire wealthy (or at least reasonably well prepared).

Unfortunately, regardless of how many books we've read, successfully reaching our financial retirement goals is still hard. Really hard.

Americans' biggest financial or money-management regret? *Not having saved enough during active working years!* The Economic Policy Institute[4] is blunt about our lack of savings: The median savings for families whose wage earners are now between 40 and 55 is … $8,000. For those between ages 56 and 61, it is … $17,000. See how far from the amounts on the previous age-specific savings chart these sums are? What is worse, how fast would you spend either of those amounts when you retire, when your current wage or salary income is gone? I can hear some of you laughing. And others crying …[5]

Americans' biggest financial or money-management regret? Not having saved enough during active working years!

Even worse, let's imagine that you've taken your financial future back into your own hands and you've finally started saving more aggressively when you are, say, in your late 40s. Those financial advisors never mention just how much more difficult it becomes to achieve a financial savings goal once we get really behind, notably once we enter our middle-aged years (our 40s and 50s). In later chapters, I share more details about why this is so difficult, and what we can do about it.

My point is this: If you aren't on track for achieving your savings goal, you aren't alone. Please understand that you are sitting in a very, very big boat with others!

Also understand that it's not all your fault. There are a number of factors, many outside your control, working against you and your retirement objectives.

Just to be clear, there is no "big-brother conspiracy" against us. However, it is a fact that institutions and corporations systematically plan and operate with their own self-interests in mind – not yours or mine. These organizations are fundamentally incapable of contemplating the effects their internal profit-driven plans and strategies may have on your ability to retire in the future. The sooner you understand this, the faster you can work to avoid the common retirement planning pitfalls surrounding you on all sides.

Let's start with a few of the more notable challenges working against your retirement interest:

- U.S. government dysfunction. This makes it increasingly difficult for you to collect your fair share of Social Security, as the government raises the eligibility age requirement, and citizens are concerned about the solvency of the social security fund. And how do we know they are investing and growing our social security contributions wisely, when we have no say in the matter?
- Corporate pensions. En masse, large businesses/ corporations are discontinuing their support for any type of pension program, or outright reneging on pension payout terms for eligible retirees within their programs.
- Corporations embracing 401(k)s. These tax-favored programs have been offered as a suitable retirement savings alternative, but in reality, the programs push the financial burden and most of the risks from the "sponsoring" employers over to you.
- The financial services industry. This industry's persistent attempts to exploit Main Street investors (you and me) with hidden and exorbitant fees are as outrageous as they are unavoidable. In addition, they will use insider information and exploit closed-door deal-making to grab market opportunities for their own wealth expansion … and to your detriment.

- Big consumer lending businesses. Big consumer credit companies like Visa or Mastercard advertise explicitly to discourage you from saving and they even incentivize ever-expanding, never-ending consumer debt to increase their own profits ... making your retirement-saving efforts even harder.
- Wall Street protectionism. The financial services industry (aka Wall Street) systematically blocks all attempts by the outraged public or the federal government itself to reform its often-covert ways of doing business. It also successfully lobbies away any attempt at enforcement of consumer protection laws (e.g., Dodd-Frank) that would help prevent economic calamities. Thus, we see "too big to fail" as an excuse used by the federal government for propping up the industry with billions of our dollars ... totally ignoring that the common, everyday person's savings have just been stolen out from under his or her nose.
- The healthcare industry. This industry is hugely successful at continuously increasing your insurance premium rates and refusing to pay for an ever-lengthening list of services. This results in the industry capturing an ever-increasing share of dollars out of your wallet for overpriced healthcare-related services.

If it ever crossed your mind that these institutions and corporate entities have little regard for your financial future, you are correct. They don't benefit from you being able to successfully and fully fund your own retirement! In most cases, your success conflicts directly with their success, so they are not about to change their ways just to help you out.

Regardless of these challenges, if you are aware of the barriers and become well-informed beyond the reduced, incomplete information these institutions wish you to know, you can still achieve your dream retirement. You just need accurate information to lead you to the right strategy that will empower you to break through these seemingly sizable barriers.

I am passionate about your success at funding and living out a great retirement! I really want you to experience the retirement of your dreams. I suspect you have an exciting vision for what your post-retirement lifestyle should be, and I bet it doesn't include barely getting by financially or asking customers, "Would you like fries with that?" If I'm right, I strongly encourage you to read this book in its entirety. It will offer you a radical new approach for finally getting your retirement plan on track, *regardless* of your current financial circumstances.

Before we discuss how to successfully achieve your dream retirement, it's important to first understand the retirement planning trap many of us have fallen victim to.

The Retirement Dilemma

Many obstacles exist that prevent us from achieving our Dream Retirement, and I've already shown you several of them. As we age, most of us are likely to encounter similar challenges at each major stage of our lives. These stages and their respective challenges are what I collectively refer to as "***The Retirement Dilemma.***"

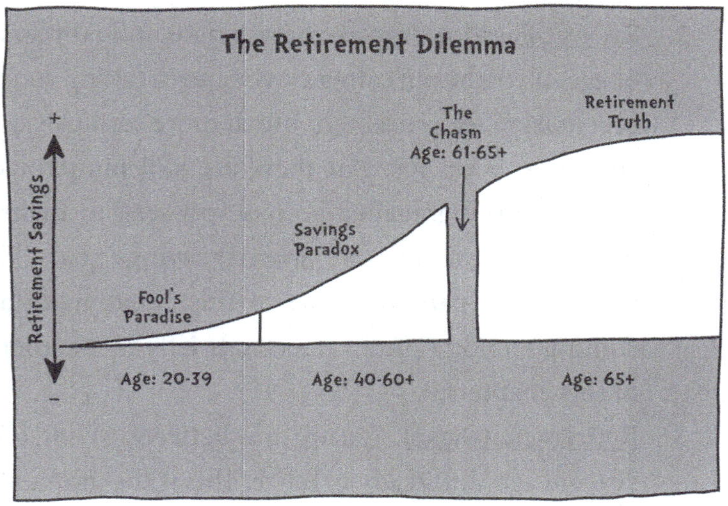

From age 20 when most of you entered the workforce, to your mid-60s when most of you will leave it or at least wish to, you are, in fact, working your way through each of four distinct stages of the Retirement Dilemma. Each one is a part of your journey to retirement. Each of the stages will, in its own way, influence the quality of your retirement.

Those stages are:

1. Fool's Paradise. You are between 20 and 39 years of age. Saving for retirement simply isn't as high a priority for you at this age, even though financial experts encourage us to begin saving early and continuously. In fact, and this is where the "paradise" part of your foolishness comes in, saving for retirement hasn't been in your vocabulary! Your ignorance is bliss … for a while longer.
2. Savings Paradox. You are between 40 and 60 years of age. If you haven't already, you begin taking your preparation for retirement much more seriously as you enter your 40s. But there are still numerous factors working against you as you seek to make up for lost time in your original savings goal. I'll explain the "paradox" part of this equation in a coming section (Hint: I referred briefly to it earlier in this chapter).
3. Retirement Chasm. You are now between 61 and 65 years of age, and ready to retire. This is the moment of truth, when you realize that yes, you are ready to retire in many ways, but still thinking, "Oh my gosh, am I financially able to retire?" This is when, at long last, you're forced to reconcile your retirement *vision* with your financial *reality* … and you identify a potentially big, cavernous gap or chasm between the two.
4. Retirement Truth. You are 65 years of age or older.

> You get a hard, brutal look at your post-retirement lifestyle and finally understand how it is likely to be from here on out. Good, bad or indifferent, you must embrace your retirement truth – because it is now what you are waking up to every morning. You do have a choice: You can live the lifestyle your finances will support, often just settling for what you have … or you can decide to delay retirement altogether (meaning going back to work).

Let's spend time looking at each stage in detail and understanding how we're taught to approach retirement planning … and how it contrasts with what we actually do.

Fool's Paradise Stage

This is when you are between 20 and 39 years of age. Once you enter your 20s – your transition into adulthood – you are likely to experience the time of your life! Enjoying your new freedom away from Mom and Dad and away from the constraints of a college campus life. Enjoying everything life has to offer out in the world. Not saving any money, even though you may earmark some of your earnings to pay down debt. Ignoring, or at least denying, the potential trouble that comes from not taking a realistic look at the financial side of the world …

aka not "saving enough money regularly" for the future or even for a rainy day.

At this stage, for many of you, saving for retirement just isn't a priority. Worse, those words, "saving for retirement" are just not part of your vocabulary. It might as well be white noise or static crackling in your ears! For those no-to-slow savers, there are typically good reasons for not saving. In your 20s and 30s, you tend to prioritize:

- Paying off debts, notably student loans or that car, and saying, "Hey! That was just a huge chunk of my income right there!"
- Exploring life, and realizing that, "Hey! It costs money."
- Finding a mate, and thinking, "Hey! Dating isn't cheap."
- Establishing a family, and saying, "Hey! (you get the idea)."

But perhaps the single greatest impediment to saving is actually not on that list; it's a *psychological one.*

It is "*disconnection.*" Not disconnection from people, but from your decades-distant future. The younger you are, the more difficult it is to connect with or visualize your future life. Four or five decades down the road is an eternity at this young age. You have a hard time envisioning yourself as an older or retired person during the far-off future years … or even as an adult in your mid-40s!

Various studies have proven the existence of this mindset, such as the 2016 Prudential Challenge Quiz, where 56 percent of the adults who participated agreed that they could not picture themselves in their older years. Some have termed this *The Longevity Disconnect Bias*, and as a result, you convince yourself that you have plenty of time stretching out ahead of you to save for those retirement years. You delude yourself into believing you have time, when in reality, you have to start saving massively for retirement – and do so on the double.

With this bias and your various other priorities all firmly occupying your attention, you make little to no progress toward saving for retirement. This lack of financial-savings progress deeply contradicts the advice expressed by those financial planners I talked about earlier. I personally remember financial advisors recommending to me that I "save for retirement straight, up, and to the right." I present that in the following graph:

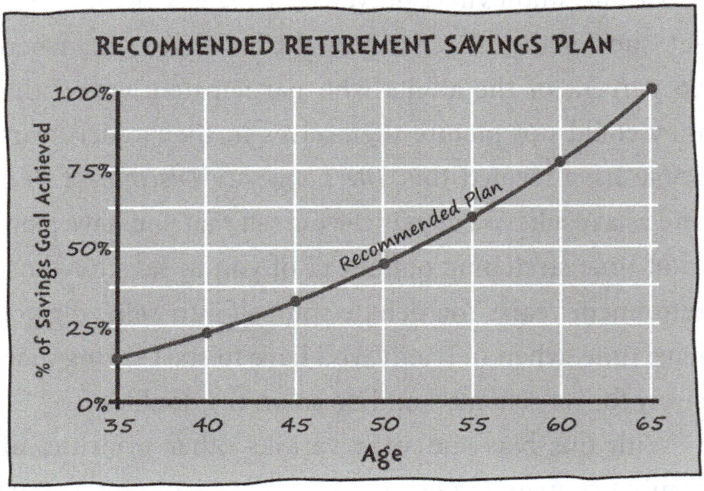

If you successfully achieved your savings goals at the ages noted in my age-specific savings chart at the beginning of this chapter, and plotted those data points on a graph, your retirement trajectory would resemble the upward, modestly arcing line illustrated above. It is a straight line, moving up, and to the right all the time.

The experts consider this trajectory to be the ideal retirement savings path. I refer to this approach as the "Recommended Plan" for retirement savings. Recommended, aka theoretical, because I have met few real people who have done it!

Looking back years later, most people regret not having a (or not implementing a better) savings strategy during this Fool's Paradise stage, and as a result they become much more serious and focused as they move on to the next stage.

However, to successfully retire, you need practical solutions to start moving in a different, retirement-building direction.

Savings Paradox Stage

Life goes on. You age. You are between 40 and 60 years of age.

You 'outgrow' the Fool's Paradise as you enter your 40s. Many of you, due to real-life circumstances, are not on track with your savings. You may not even be clear on how to connect the dots to achieve the retirement lifestyle you deserve.

Anxiety about the future is growing, and you are not happy with your immediate options to retire successfully. You become increasingly drawn back, time and again, to the *need* to build your savings, and you might even guilt-trip yourself about your lack of savings and the absence of a savings habit.

You may not have paid down personal debts; you may not be in full control of your debt spending. But you have the growing sense that you've already lost precious time. Your sense of urgency to "save for retirement" has gone up dramatically.

By this time, you are contemplating and pursuing much more aggressive strategies to grow your retirement funds in order to catch up to your original savings goal before it's too late and the time to retire is upon you.

I refer to this Savings Paradox period as your "catch-up time" – the time to aggressively build your retirement savings amount. You are behind on your savings plan, no doubt. To still achieve your original retirement savings goal, you become hyper-aggressive in saving money, earning money, and/or increasing the return on your investments. You put a lot of hope and faith into your plan, since you seem to have few other options.

If your plan fails, you may have to consider either delaying your retirement or lowering your standard of living during retirement. Neither option is ideal, and you perhaps reject both. After all, you may say (as you fall back on the Fool's Paradise mindset), "I have time and don't have to decide right now."

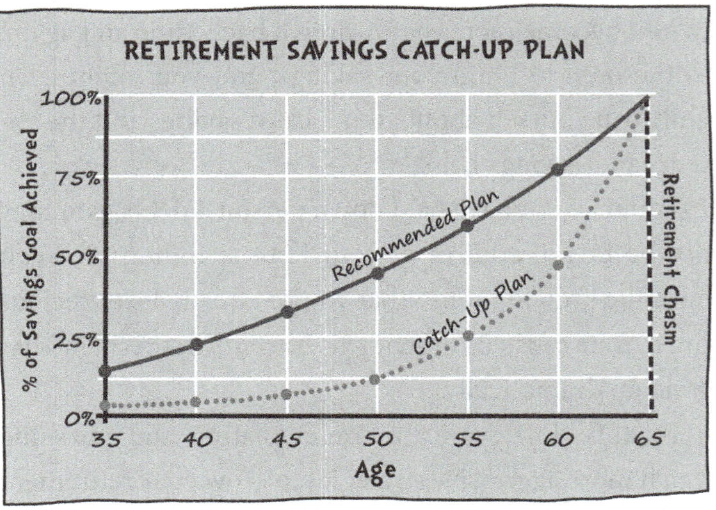

If you plot on a new graph what a Retirement Savings Catch-Up Plan looks like, it tends to resemble the chart above. In your 20s, 30s and sometimes your 40s, your savings lag behind what financial experts recommend … or frankly they are at zero. In your 40s and 50s, you begin to become much more assertive in your retirement planning and saving. You hope to reach your savings goal just in time for your mid-60s retirement.

If you have embraced a catch-up strategy, you have no choice but to be optimistic, positive and fiercely determined in your plan to achieve that retirement funding goal. Failure isn't an option.

But as you take a closer, more realistic look at your path to success, you must be honest: You have a lot of ground to make up in a relatively short time frame! You have to save more money in your 50s than you ever had to in your 20s. For every dollar you didn't save in your 20s, you'll need to save three to five dollars more in your 50s and 60s to make up the difference – *and you get uncomfortable just reading those words, don't you?*

For every dollar you didn't save in your 20s, you'll need to save three to five dollars more in your 50s and 60s to make up the difference.

Doing this becomes no small feat when you consider the fact that changing your savings trajectory becomes even more difficult with age. More difficult? I'll explain in the next chapter.

Retirement Chasm Stage

Time, as they say, waits for no one. You are between 61 and 65 years of age.

Imagine you're approaching 60, and you see no way that you can achieve your savings goal by your actual retirement from the workforce, be it at age 62 or 65. The idea of completely catching up seems unrealistic now and you begin to question, if you hadn't already, whether you should even hope to close the savings gap between your financial plan and the reality of your income needs in retirement. You are facing a big, gaping chasm.

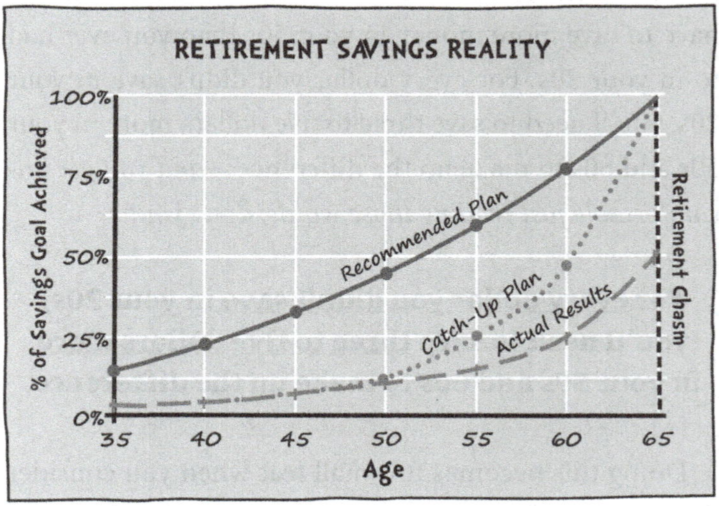

The above chart highlights the difference between where you should be according to financial advisors (Recommended Plan line), where you hoped you'd be (Catch-up Plan line) and where you really are (Actual Results line). (Many of you are nodding along and saying, "Yes, this is true! How did you know?")

Let's look at the state of things at the age of 65. You have reached your retirement age. You must make important life decisions. You were supposed to have successfully achieved 100 percent of your retirement savings goal by now, and left the world of work to embark on this new adventure called retirement. However, as the Actual Results line in the chart illustrates, you've only satisfied 50 percent of your savings goal (see that vertical Retirement Chasm line and the bottom dashed line that intersects with it), meaning your retirement years are only half-funded!

Unfortunately, missing a retirement goal by 50 percent or more is a common reality, with half of American families without any retirement account money at all.

It's no wonder that the retirement results for many Americans diverge significantly from the plan recommended by experts. A catch-up plan is aggressive in its attempt to make up for lost time. It's based on best-case-scenario assumptions (which rarely materialize) and as a result many fail to ever reach their original savings goals.[6] In contrast, the Purchase Power Retirement Formula presents a realistic, attainable method of preparing for retirement, no matter what stage you are in right now.

CHAPTER 2:

THE NATURE OF YOUR CHALLENGE

Regardless of how successful you believe you will be in achieving your retirement goal, the truth is that saving aggressively and attempting to catch up in later years is difficult, and as I discussed in the last chapter, it creates a savings paradox. It is complicated by various challenges associated with aging, which make it harder to successfully make more money, save more money, and maximize your ROI.

I know many people who refuse to believe that age is anything more than an arbitrary number! However, even though people have a greater urgency to grow their retirement savings, there are real, age-related obstacles that cause them to fail with their catch-up plans, and eventually they settle for what becomes their reality or actual results.

These real barriers make successfully catching up and achieving your retirement savings goal difficult. Keep in mind the obstacles are common to all of us.

Less Runway

Imagine this: You are sitting in an airplane preparing for takeoff, and the pilot informs you that a good-sized portion of the airport runway has just been damaged and is only partially available. What goes through your mind? Personally, I would think there's no way the plane could take off safely, and I'd deplane and find a safer way to my destination!

This is like saving for retirement, where the length of your runway is key to your ability to successfully reach your savings goal. In effect, if you are 40 or older, you have lost all the runway that your 20s and 30s represented. You have lost two or more decades of "runway."

Saving for retirement starting in your early 20s provides that long runway. It allows you to spread your savings goal and any unforeseen risk over a 45-year timeframe. If you wait until your 40s to begin saving, you'll have a much shorter runway (15-20 years shorter) to ramp up your savings and benefit from compounding returns. You'll also have a shorter runway to financially recover from any unforeseen financial or economic challenges that might still occur on your way to your retirement years.

Unforeseen challenges? Yes. Think stock market crash, mortgage/international financial industry crises and spiking unemployment as just three examples of challenges we have all witnessed in the past century alone. Imagine (and some of you just need to think back a few short years) that any of the following events may occur while you are aggressively saving for retirement:

- The stock market experiences an unprecedented decline.
- You are demoted, moved from full-time to part-time, or laid off.
- The economy enters a recession and your industry of employment is severely affected.
- You experience a major personal or family emergency that gobbles up your savings.
- The real estate or mortgage financing market crashes, and with it, your home's value; your equity in the property might vanish overnight.
- Your credit card debt balloons to over $40,000.

The closer you are to retirement, the less time you'll have to fully recover from any of these financially devastating events. Any one of these cyclical and common events could have a debilitating effect on your plan for funding your retirement.

Business and industry expands and contracts, and we know there are times of great unemployment just as there are times with plenty of jobs. The stock market index goes up, then down, then back up, over and over again. Economists and historians join in telling us that the U.S. has experienced 47 recessions in its history. Forty-seven! If they last on average about two years, that's 94 years of our national history in recession … This effectively means that we will experience more than one recession in our lifetime. During a recession, much wealth is lost or spent, and we start all over again – to earn, save and invest. We are nothing if not tenacious!

The recession of 2007 lasted seven quarters – officially. I know some who'd say we simply *never* bounced back, even now, over a decade later. During that time our combined household wealth plummeted from $65 trillion to approximately $49 trillion. A chunk of that loss was embedded in our real estate – the value of our homes.

For many who had planned to retire anytime from 2007 to, say, 2010, their retirement funds were down the tubes. If you were within a few years of retiring during that recession, you likely considered either delaying retirement or dramatically reducing your lifestyle during retirement – or both, in order to preserve and hopefully rebuild those accounts.

So, we see that the first obstacle is that a portion of our runway disappears out from under us. Less time for saving. Less recovery time in the case of any financial, savings-devouring crisis.

The Peaking Effect

We all imagine that we'll be earning the "most ever in our careers" in the years *just before we retire.* Beware! It is a myth! Statistical observation shows this assumption to be false!

It's a myth that we earn the most in our careers just before we retire.

Our next obstacle in our 40s and 50s is all about the "peaking effect." Your *earnings trajectory* is not continuously upward, contrary to common expectations. Income and earnings potential *peak* at an earlier age than you may think. That is an obstacle if one of your approaches to a better retirement is making more money (which you must save) later in life. According to a February 2015 report by the Federal Reserve Bank of New York:

- By their mid-50s, men are making about 127 percent more than when just starting out in their careers.

That sounds optimistic, doesn't it? But here's the distressing clincher:

- On average, most men's earnings top out at about age 48.

This *average* includes men in both white-collar and blue-collar jobs. In fact, the latter – as a result of declining physical capabilities at work – see wage earnings decline earlier than white-collar men. But none are exempt.

- Women's pay tends to peak even younger, at age 39-40.

This may partially be due to parental absences for childbearing and child-rearing. It is also most certainly due to women's persistently lower earnings than men for the same work performed. The gender bias of the infamous glass ceiling is still present in the workplace, and women seem to need to have broken through that ceiling fairly young … or it won't happen at all. Not breaking upward through that barrier means earnings stagnate up to a decade sooner than for men.[7]

That is not what we expected while in our 20s, nor at any point of our lives, really. Not being able to earn more in our later active years in the workforce due to the obstacle called the peaking effect is most assuredly a big obstacle to saving more, but not the final one.

Employment Insecurity

Securing and maintaining employment becomes more challenging with age any time when job-changing is in the cards.

Although it is against the law of the land to discriminate based on age in our workplaces, the fact of the matter is that post-recession ageism, or bias against older-aged workers, is real. Employers hire younger workers because they are, arguably, just as educated as older workers – and much cheaper. In times of reductions in any workforce (called RIFs by those who engineer them), it will always be a case of the older, more expensive workers going first. And try to find another job afterward ... I dare you! During your 40s and 50s, job insecurity – and the inability to earn just as much or more in the new job as in the old – is a very real block to knowing how much you can save toward your retirement.

Unemployment leads to us digging into our savings far, far too often rather than building them. Here is why:

- Median monthly earnings decline 23 percent after an unemployment spell for unemployed workers aged 50 to 61, compared with just 11 percent for workers aged 25 to 34, according to a recent Urban Institute report.
- For workers 62 and older, post-unemployment earnings plummet to nearly half (47 percent), although most of the decline in that age group stems from a shift toward part-time employment.
- "For many workers laid off during and after the Great Recession [of the 21st century], the financial ramifications of job loss may persist for the rest of their lives," according to the report, *Age Disparities in Unemployment and Reemployment During the Great Recession and Recovery*, by Richard W. Johnson and Barbara A. Butrica.
- The same study also showed that it took more than nine months of job searching for half of unemployed adults aged 50 to 61 to find work, compared to six months for adults aged 25 to 34, and seven months for adults aged 35 to 49.

- Adults 62 and older who lost their jobs were the least likely age group to find work – only about a third (34 percent) found jobs within a year.
- Perhaps most troubling, half of adults 62 and older dropped out of the labor force entirely (stopped seeking work, and therefore were no longer part of federal job-seekers/employment data collection) within nine months of losing work.[8]

Conservative Investing

As we age, financial advisors encourage us to invest in more conservative instruments. This word "conservative" simply means "it earns you less" as a result of taking less financial risk.

Why do I count conservative investing as an obstacle? After all, you say, "I am saving and investing!" Increasing your savings through lower interest or gains on your chosen investments is slower – you'll need more runway length, more years – than with other fast-growing types of investments. But we've just seen that you don't have more years because your runway is shortened! While this conservative approach doesn't take you where you need to be financially, you have limited options since you must be increasingly more risk-averse as you age, to protect your existing nest egg.

Debt

I would hope that "debt" is clearly understood as an obstacle to saving more. If you had no debt, you could take all that money you're using to pay down debt and instead plow it into a retirement fund!

There is some good news: Household debt levels start to decline for householders between ages 45 and 54. Yet, the average debt for people in this age bracket is still an astounding $150,500! Between the ages of 55 and 64, when we should be "free and clear" and have plush retirement accounts, our average debt levels still stand at $131,900![9]

Frankly, it is easy to say we'd all prefer to have that amount of cash earning a tidy interest rate in our retirement accounts, but that is not our reality. What a huge obstacle debt is for us! One of the bigger reasons Americans don't save enough is because of our levels of personal (aka consumer) debt. Our "free cash" is going to pay off our debts, rather than piling up as a growing principle earning a good interest rate (or dividends or profits) in a nice retirement nest-egg.

It's probably not a coincidence that the average salary for those in this age bracket is the highest for any age bracket, but that never means such a large amount of debt is a good thing. We might have assets in excess of this debt, true; on the other hand, we might have negative net worth. In short, for some in this age group, lingering debt can be a reason to postpone retirement.

All debt is an obstacle to saving more cash for retirement.

The biggest wealth-creation step you can take is to become debt-free. This means you don't owe anyone any money and all your earnings are yours. It means you have more free and clear cash to save and invest.

We have $3.8 trillion dollars in consumer debt in the U.S. This is only our household or personal debt – not business or government debt. What comprises this consumer debt? Mortgages! The idea behind those 30-year loans is that you buy your residence in your 20s when you start earning money, and the loan is paid off in your 50s – well before you retire. But will that be true?

Credit cards, auto loans and school loans are the next big consumer debts we carry around as a nation. Credit cards are real debt when you cannot (or simply don't) pay them down in full each month. When you don't pay them off, you also pay lots of interest – more in a year than you probably know.

We resist calculating our own personal debt. The interest we pay on our auto loans, credit card balances and other debt servicing could be equal to one or more months of our net pay! That is cash we could be socking away for retirement. Somehow, we prefer to give it to the bank or the credit card company. We resist creating and following a determined plan to get rid of debt, and thus those interest payments. It puts our retirement in peril.

Challenges Create Urgency

So, you see that there are a number of challenges associated with aggressively saving money as we get older. The longer we wait to focus on our retirement savings plan, the more susceptible we are to these obstacles.

While we have more urgency and focus to save for retirement in our 40s and 50s than ever before, there are also more obstacles and barriers than at any prior age to successfully saving money, and you find yourself experiencing the savings paradox.

Time is now of the essence; you are getting closer and closer to your retirement date.

What can you do when you are near retirement and realize that you have missed your retirement goal by 25 percent, 50 percent … or more? If previous generations before us are any indication, you'll be forced to quickly accept your financial reality and the limited options available.

Again, these options are to:

1) Delay retirement. Postpone your retirement date (decision made while still employed) and keep working to increase the amount of your retirement savings.

2) Downsize retirement. Retire on time but lower your standard of living and lifestyle (spending) to fall within your smaller financial means.
3) Forgo retirement. Never retire, and work as long as you physically and mentally can do so.

We'll discuss these retirement options in depth in a later chapter, but the vital thing to understand is that this retirement planning pattern of getting behind early (Fool's Paradise) and unsuccessfully seeking to play catch up (Savings Paradox) is common … and growing as the retirement crisis deepens. This dynamic has become so popular that I studied it extensively and gave it a name, "The Retirement Chasm." It is when you look at your retirement savings, calculate if you will be able to live on that amount for the totality of your retirement years … and see a deep, empty gap between the lifestyle you want and the one you can afford.

A Retirement Chasm is when a significant gap exists between your projected retirement savings and your retirement goal.

This stage of your retirement journey can be one of the most stressful times of life that you ever experience. That is because you are forced to accept your financial reality and acknowledge that it does not correspond with your hopes and dreams. It becomes a moment of reckoning. A rude wake-up call. It is – with no further ado – the time to acknowledge and accept your retirement options and the truth. Imagine when the retirement you've dreamed about is replaced with the prospects of living near the poverty line, or worse, never retiring at all …

For some, retirement will be a time of great joy and happiness, particularly if they met or exceeded their financial goals. They can now leap across the chasm with a spring in their step and begin enjoying the lifestyle they always dreamed of for their later years.

• RETIREMENT CHASM •

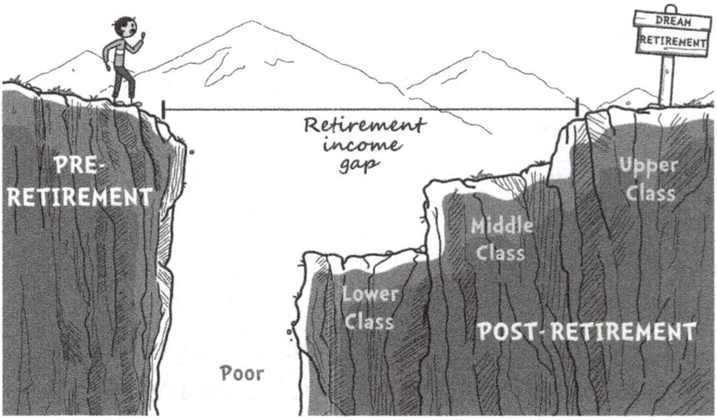

The Retirement Chasm, shown above, is defined by two distinct cliffs – the left-side's pre-retirement and the right-side's post-retirement are separated by a significant distance. The expanse between the cliffs represents how much you need to save for retirement. While you want your version of the dream retirement to materialize for you, <u>where</u> you actually land when you jump off the pre-retirement cliff depends directly on the size of your retirement income gap and how much you have saved for retirement.

Where Will You Land?

Retirement – or crossing the chasm – offers four post-retirement landing spots. Each one is a distinct retirement lifestyle. Where will you land when you take that leap into your actual retirement?

Each landing place represents a specific standard of living and quality of life you could experience during retirement. To illustrate this chasm more clearly, I'm taking a brief detour into "socio-economic classes" during retirement. They are shown in the above image as:

- Poor (where you just keep falling)
- Lower class (a great degree of struggle)
- Middle class (less struggle, but not the life perhaps desired)
- Upper class (all is well in your perfect world for your Dream Retirement)

The goal as you approach retirement should be to either maintain or increase your pre-retirement socio-economic class. That means if you were middle class during your working years, you should strive to achieve a middle or upper class lifestyle after you retire. We all dread dropping down a level, but in reality many Americans who haven't adequately prepared find themselves going down a level as they are forced to reduce their living expenses to preserve their retirement savings.

Your goal when approaching retirement should always be to maintain, or better yet to improve, your standard of living and quality of life.

Poor Lifestyle

This level equates to living at or below the national poverty line of income during your retirement years. To be at the poverty line means you either struggle mightily or are outright unable to take care of all your basic necessities – food, housing, transportation and clothing.

The poor class, often without a strong education, is typified by poverty, homelessness, and few, if any, assets. People in this class might suffer a lack of medical care, or struggle to obtain/pay for adequate housing and enough or good-quality food, climate-appropriate clothing.

Lower Class Lifestyle

This class of person may live in rental housing or non-luxury housing. They have just enough to take care of their basic necessities, but not much more than that. This household lives paycheck-to-paycheck, and struggles mightily to save a reasonable amount of money for retirement.

During retirement they are likely to rely solely on social security, may have to continue working part- or full-time to sustain themselves.

Middle Class Lifestyle

In the middle class, people have a greater educational background – high school, college, or trade/vocational school education or degree. They have more income available for consumption and may own property. Those in the middle class often are employed as professionals, managers and civil servants. We might say that there is a "lower" middle class and an "upper" middle class, though not all of our institutions look at it that way.

Regional disparities in income and the cost of living mean that salary-based measures of the middle class can vary greatly. Thus, this group ends up being (statistically, anyway) the largest population in the land.

While it is assumed that middle class households generate sufficient income for retirement savings along with their ability to cover standard expenses, an increasing segment of this portion of the American population is also living paycheck-to-paycheck. This is simply a term meaning "just enough to meet the bills" and it eliminates the ability to save.

Upper Class Lifestyle

Comprising only 1 to 3 percent of the United States population, the upper class holds more than 25 percent of the nation's wealth.

Those in this upper-class segment typically have more money than they could spend in their lifetimes, which leaves them with a great deal of leisure time for cultivating a variety of interests. As might be expected, they also exercise influence and power both nationally and globally.

Crossing the Chasm

Crossing the Retirement Chasm comes with tremendous risk and great shock for those who are unprepared, especially when forced to land in a lower socio-economic class due to their financial reality.

For instance, while you may have maintained a middle-class standard of living during your pre-retirement active years, things might be about to change. Crossing the chasm introduces the risk that your previous standard of living may <u>decline</u>. This leap across the chasm has you moving downward into a lower-class level than during your active, working years. Where you end up depends on how financially prepared you are for retirement.

Crossing the chasm introduces the risk that your previous standard of living may *decline.*

In the prior illustration, we saw a person at the top of the pre-retirement cliff seeking to cross the chasm and reach his Dream Retirement. However, the individual cannot just jump all the way across from that cliff and land at the top of the opposite cliff. Leaping is dangerous and would at best mean falling straight down into the chasm of a poorer-class experience.

Crossing the Retirement Chasm successfully is all about transitioning from pre-retirement to post-retirement while <u>maintaining or improving your quality of life and standard of living.</u>

I equate the achievement of your ideal Dream Retirement to *your own brand* of upper-class living. It is the highest level you can achieve and allows you to experience all of the benefits and advantages you'd expect with a first-class retirement lifestyle.

To successfully cross the chasm into that higher lifestyle, you require a bridge, since jumping across is not an option. The bridge is composed of the typical retirement income components we've all heard about: Social Security, pensions and personal savings (savings which might include CDs, 401(k)s, IRAs, investment real estate, and so on). The bridge is only as long as the amount of your retirement savings.

This means a post-retirement lifestyle for one individual may equate to a lower-class lifestyle, while for someone else it may equate to an upper-middle-class one.

Crossing the Retirement Chasm is about maintaining or improving your quality of life and standard of living during retirement.

• RETIREMENT CHASM •

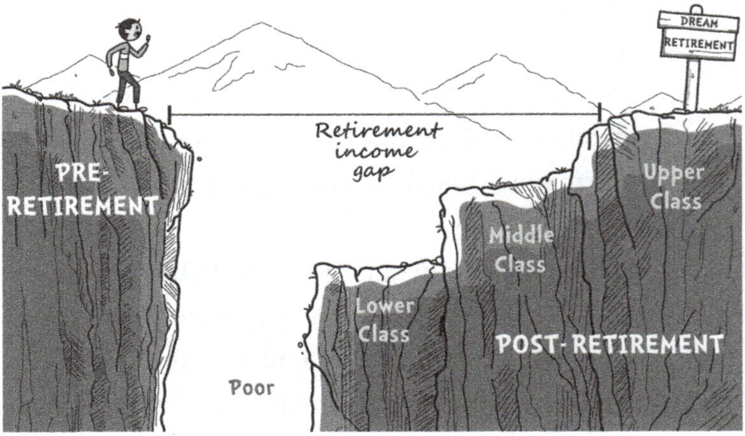

The Retirement Chasm illustration presents a journey across the chasm that is important for us all to understand. I will reference it throughout this book to highlight the various ways people seek to retire as they attempt to reconcile their retirement vision with their financial reality.

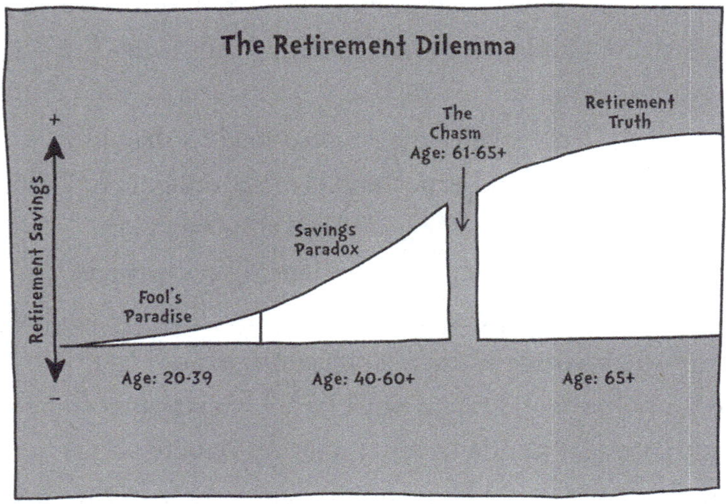

If you recall from Chapter 1, we discussed the first three stages of the Retirement Dilemma: Fool's Paradise, Savings Paradox and Retirement Chasm. Now let's discuss the final stage: Retirement Truth.

Retirement Truth Stage

Time has marched on and you are now fully in your post-age-65 retirement. This Retirement Truth stage is your in-retirement reality.

For some of you, it will not represent as dramatic a lifestyle shift as you feared, but you will nonetheless find that some changes are still required. Some may find that a simple shift in one or two of your past expenses does the trick. Others might delay retirement just an additional year or two – continuing to earn and to save aggressively – and then move into retirement with a greater peace of mind.

For others, it will be best described as dismally below your hopes and expectations of retirement. You will be asking yourself, "For *this* I worked for 40 years?" You may retire in spite of it all, experiencing a downsized and significantly compromised lifestyle. It will be a reality of monetary struggle, mental frustration and emotional disappointment. Others won't be able to stay this course and may just decide to forgo their retirement altogether and go back to working and earning as long as they are able … somehow.

If you are currently behind on your retirement savings goal without real, viable solutions, your retirement truth will seem increasingly bleak to you. As you find your attempts to aggressively save more are financially yielding less and less of the savings results you hoped for, you must face the truth of an inferior post-retirement lifestyle.

The Key Is Maximizing Savings

If you are under the age of 50 or otherwise know that you have more than 15 years before you plan to retire, I encourage you to continue pursuing strategies for:

1. Making more money
2. Saving more money
3. Generating higher returns (profits and growth) from your invested savings

The more you can leverage (extend and use) time to close your retirement funding gap, the better off you will be later on when you apply the Purchase Power Retirement Formula (PPRF) I discuss in later chapters of this book.

If you are over 50, you are probably all too aware of the challenges of significantly changing your retirement savings trajectory. Your retirement plan probably has little to no margin for error and little wiggle room to reposition investments to earn more profits faster. While it is critical that you continue to pursue income-generating and savings-related strategies, you'll need to begin considering retirement strategies that take into account the reality of retiring with a notable gap in income or savings.

Just to be clear, this book will not teach you how to make more money, save more money, or increase your investment returns. There are plenty of books available to help you dramatically (and innovatively) improve in each of those areas. My book will teach you how to ***maximize or leverage*** *your retirement savings, however much it ends up being*. Whether it is less than $100,000, about $300,000, or $1,000,000 or more, there are ways to maximize and stretch those dollars.

I will show you how to maximize your retirement savings, however much it ends up being.

Whatever your financial circumstances, the second part of this book will introduce and discuss leveraging principles, based on the Purchase Power Retirement Formula, which will help you maximize and leverage your retirement savings and income. The principles that the Formula is based on have existed for a long time but have seldom been extensively researched or discussed as a *strategy for retirement*.

The Purchase Power Retirement Formula can serve as the perfect complement to your existing financial strategy. Think of it as another tool in your financial and retirement planning toolkit, if you will. It can be applied to successfully enable the retirement experience you deserve.

Before launching ourselves into the Formula itself, let's examine where we are with our collective and individual retirement funding options. I'll review the history of the American retirement funding system and show how the "powers that be" sincerely tried to help Americans fund a secure retirement. Then we'll see how those "best laid plans" were thwarted – how the modern-day retirement crisis was born and continues to unfold even today.

This is important because it gives you the framework from which you have been or will be working to fund your retirement. By doing this study, we also gain an understanding about why many post-baby boomer generations will (still) find it difficult to achieve their dream retirements.

CHAPTER 3:

A BRIEF HISTORY OF THE (BROKEN) RETIREMENT FUNDING SYSTEM

No complex system – such as federal tax systems and their later reforms, or new legislation to regulate a brand-new industry like the internet or World Wide Web – is created in one board meeting or in one session of Congress. As you might guess, our retirement funding system is one of those complex creatures that has evolved over several decades. Let's look at how the system emerged, expanded and is now disintegrating.

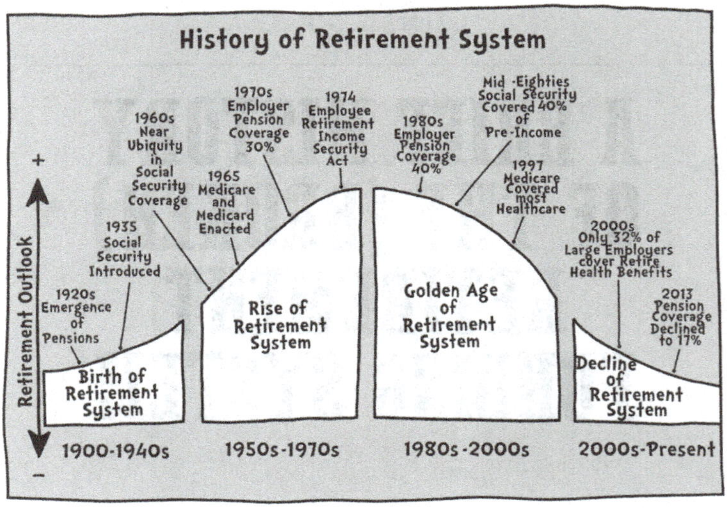

The Birth of our Retirement System – 1900-1940s

Struggle was a key aspect of life in the late 19th and early 20th centuries, for several reasons. A number of events happened during this long period, often simultaneously:

- The Industrial Revolution and its employers were ready for an overhaul in how they treated workers – that was the view of the workers! The Workers Union movements begun after the Civil War took on renewed energy in the early 20th century.
- Two 20th-century world wars killed tens of millions. So many who came home were disabled,

unable to work and needed financial help – as did their families.

- To add insult to injury, right on the heels of World War I (WWI), millions more died in the Spanish influenza epidemic, leaving many more families decimated and in need of support.
- Just before World War II (WWII), our elders struggled through the worst economic Depression ever known in our post-Industrial Revolution economy. Between the two World Wars, in the 1930s, the movement for new labor legislation again picked up steam – both in Europe and the United States.
- And then WWII was upon us and, as after WWI, our soldiers came home wounded, weary and disabled. Again, Americans by the millions needed help. Desperate times indeed …

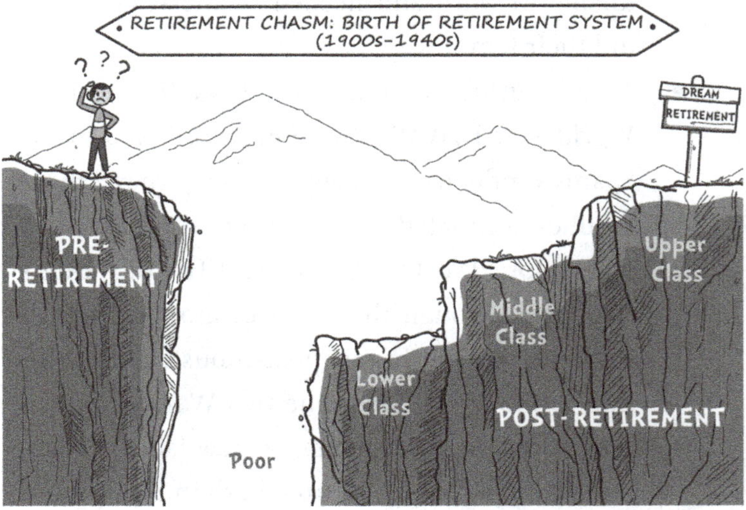

Before any retirement funding system (government or employer-sponsored) existed, *families* were the fallback system of old-age support, or support in the case of long-term disability or illness. Those who could worked as long as possible, often until their death. It was typically impossible for the lower- or even mid-range wage earners to save any money or to invest in ownership of their own lodgings. That meant that when they lost their jobs, they lost their housing. People simply worked until they no longer could and most relied on family support structures to get by when they could not work.

The only aid to any part of the population – and devised exclusively for the military – was the military's pensions "for services rendered to the nation." This scheme began on the heels of the American Revolution, and compensated, for life, all soldiers who'd left active service. In our entire economy, it was all that was offered to anyone in the way of official support in times of disability or service.

So, let's imagine the "golden" years of life for an older, worn-out gentleman of that time, who worked until he couldn't work anymore, did not have a military pension of any sort, and had no supportive family members to take him in.

In other words, there was not, for the vast majority of folks, any "dream retirement" on the horizon, no time when they could kick back and enjoy the fruits of their working-year labors. There was no such fruit!

However, while retirement funding was not yet ubiquitous by the 1940s, there were clear, proven models that could now be scaled in the future.

The Rise of Our Retirement System (1950s-1970s)

It is from such a century-old history of events, unsatisfying elder-year solutions and circumstances affecting whole populations that our modern retirement funding system was born.

Baby boomers' parents – the so-called traditionalists – saw the struggle involved in these devastating events and said, "No more of *this!*" Thus, citizens collectively tried to find a way to provide for the whole population, in exchange for work whether past or present.

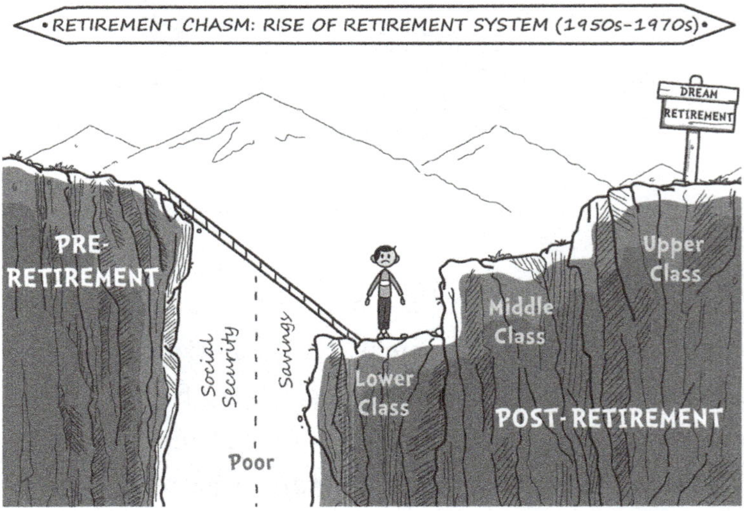

This brief history is the backdrop to how we were motivated to create a three-legged stool of funding options available to those who were active in the workforce. Between the 1930s and 1940s, we made a bit of progress, then a bit more during the 1960s and 1970s. Each successive "leg of the stool" was an essential source of income reserved for our retirement years. The legs represent income sources supported by the federal government, our employers and personal savings.

The U.S. government was under pressure for years, notably by our well-organized labor groups, to do something for ordinary workers. During the Great Depression years, it was under even more pressure to help all citizens suffering the economic downturn. What is not always known or remembered is that European countries were creating parallel programs for their constituencies, too; there was a global tide sweeping across that continent and our own due to the working populations' relentless demands.

Social Security was the result in the U.S. It was introduced in the 1930s; it applies to and benefits everyone who works. The first leg of that three-legged stool, for our purposes here, is Social Security.

Social Security

Social Security was signed into existence in August 1935 when the U.S. was deep in the Great Depression, as a "pay as you work" system. The U.S. *Title II* section of the Social Security Act that became law is what we think of as our Social Security retirement benefits today. This first leg represents the federal government managing a key source of income for those of us earning money from work. From inception, it was only ever intended (as we often hear) to be an additional or complementary source of retirement income, not the whole of it. It is, as we all know, managed by the U.S. government on our behalf. It is withdrawn by law from our paychecks before we even get our money; the principle is "what you don't have in hand, you don't spend."[10]

Voluntary Personal Savings and Investments

The second leg of our stool, personal savings, represents the individually managed income source. This was very difficult to manage for most workers until after the Great Depression of the 1930s and World War II, when incomes began to rise, banks began to be trusted again and property ownership grew rapidly with the prevalence of mortgage lending.

Post-WWII economic expansion and prosperity slowly set in, heralding a new era of full employment, salaried income and entrepreneurial opportunities. This new prosperity finally allowed individuals and households to voluntarily save some of their hard-earned money for a rainy day. What is more, they could now save for the long-term, such as for their own retirement years.

This voluntary savings leg of the stool is the most varied of the legs. Personal savings (bank savings accounts or CDs) had become a habit by the later 20th century, even when the amounts were small.

Another aspect of this savings leg which became quite common is non-financial market personal investments – additional earnings coming from investing in passive income instruments such as rental real estate, or in partnerships and outright ownership in other businesses separate from one's full-time job. These were no longer difficult or seen as odd investment choices. Side gigs and moonlighting activities for those with special skills or knowledge was and remains a common way to increase income, if only marginally for most people. Now this second leg of our three-legged retirement stool not only felt real, but was available to almost everyone.

The Golden Age of Retirement (1980s-2000s)

With two legs of our stool in place, we move into the 1980s and begin to see the third leg of our retirement funding stool take full form. It emerges in the form of pensions. This final leg helps us create a sturdy, reliable three-legged stool on which to rest and on which we could depend for our retirement funding.

Pensions

Pensions, as the third leg of our stool, are managed by our employers, and are much older than Social Security – at least in how and when they got their start. First devised for the military, the pension scheme began on the heels of the American Revolution and provided lifelong monies (though of modest amounts) for all soldiers who'd left active service. We obviously still do that for our modern career military personnel – and I personally thank you all for your service!

Much later, though, pensions were also launched in the corporate world. While the American Express corporation launched its own plan in 1875, it was eventually imitated by private sector mega-corporations. The idea slowly caught fire, with non-union employees of those mega-corporations getting pensions, just as retired unionized workers and military personnel were.

By 1960, half the American workforce had pensions, allowing them to comfortably retire with both Social Security payments and their pension payments funding their retirement years. Not only that, Medicare and Medicaid legislation was enacted in 1965 (expanded in 1997 to cover virtually all healthcare needs); this was healthcare insurance support throughout the retirement years of American retirees.

By the 1980s, we were fully ensconced in *The Golden Age* of our pension and Social Security, Medicare and Medicaid programs.[11]

Yet, I must repeat: The pension and Social Security programs were never seen as "the whole" of America's retirement funding. It was always assumed – by employers and legislators alike – that Americans were also *additionally* saving some of their earned money, with the intention of not spending it until retirement. Remember the stool's leg of personal savings. Corporate employers, encouraged by federal legislation, found a way to help us save better and more systematically. Enter the 401(k) plans to further strengthen our stool and grow our personal savings for retirement.

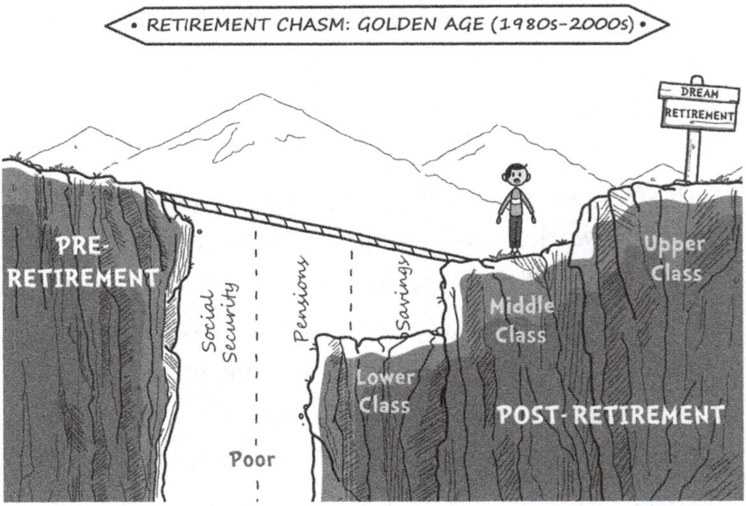

Expanded Options for Personal Saving

New opportunities for the third leg, voluntary savings, began to proliferate during this period of the 1980s and '90s, with more viable options available to the individual than ever before.

More individual investors were comfortable placing funds in the stock markets. Then, as now, stock markets experienced their highs and lows, but remained attractive to the alert and educated investor. (Quite a bit later, stock market trading accounts that you could manage, research and trade on your own came into their heyday. This was toward the end of the 1990s, with the internet and related digital technology allowing us to research our investments before choosing them – and stock brokerages creating websites allowing us to manage our own trades.)

Yet it is 401(k)s that we really think of as the centerpiece of this third voluntary savings leg of our retirement funding stool. Corporations without pension plans (non-union employers, primarily) and even many smaller companies in the private sector, started to offer something called a 401(k) tax-deferred retirement savings plan. Their decisions to do so were encouraged by new federal tax legislation, the Revenue Act of 1978.

Throughout the 1980s, 401(k)'s proliferated with that legislation mapping out how and how much we could save. These were voluntary programs for employers; they were by no means required by law to set them up for their employees. They were likewise voluntary for the employee; we could participate or not. Needless to say, workers in private-industry jobs gobbled them up. Employees enrolled by the millions when they understood the tax advantage. Participants could even decide how much to save, up to that IRS-imposed limit.

Monies in 401(k)s are invested primarily in stocks to quickly increase the value of an individual employee's saved funds. (Then and now, that has always been a volatile aspect of such plans, but has also offered the chance for great returns.)

And what was that "deferred tax" that I mentioned? The government sweetened 401(k)s and other related types of plans by making dollars saved into the plans "pre-tax" dollars, which meant that income tax would be paid later, when the money was withdrawn for retirement spending.[12]

As the 1980s came to a close, what was the picture? The U.S. had:

- Numerous private-sector, employer-sponsored and union pension plans
- Military and government/civil service pension plans
- Legislation that created 401(k)s and related types of voluntary savings programs
- A strong Social Security program

Lulled by The Golden Age of Abundance

All salaried and even self-employed workers had long paid into and earned Social Security. Those retirement payments were set to begin variously at age 62 or 65, upon one's "official" retirement from full-time employment. Ask any American what Social Security is, or how his or her pension plan or 401(k) works, and the person could tell you about the benefits.

Likewise, our ability to do our own self-directed investing of our saved cash was facilitated by technology. Individual or Main Street investors like you and me could now do more complete financial market research as the internet matured through the late 1990s and into the new century. More individual investors discovered the stock market as a source of growing their savings, and as the 1990s progressed into the new millennium and our investments rose in value, we felt pretty satisfied with our abilities to invest and grow our savings ourselves.

Added to these instruments for saving, banks were offering interest on savings and CD accounts, and we enjoyed great ease in obtaining a mortgage to earn equity as a homeowner or other real estate owner.

All these funding opportunities saw us move as a nation into the zenith, the height – The Golden Age – of the retirement system. Starting in the later 1970s and into the '80s and '90s, we came to feel quite secure in our many options to prepare for retirement.

Perhaps it was this feeling of security that led many Americans to feel that – even though they were working class and working stiffs in the literal "I work a job" sense – they could claim a place in the middle class. They felt that "middle class" meant that they would not be struggling financially during their retirement years, whereas two or three short generations ago, they would have sunk into poverty after their active working years. Now enjoying the fruits and stability of the three-legged stool for their retirement, American workers could essentially "walk" their way from their active working lives into a middle-class retirement with no fears, no panic … and no worries about healthcare. It was indeed a brand-new age for retirement in America. We could now securely transition – we could walk into our sunset years on the bridge of pensions, personal savings and Social Security.

Stable, Trusted Three-Legged Stool

We see that the U.S. now had three legs of the retirement funding stool in place:

1) The pension schemes (which, I grant you, serve only some, and are variously managed by the military, corporations or trade unions)
2) The Social Security program (which serves all Americans who are active in the workforce, and is managed by the federal government)
3) Voluntary savings: employer-administered 401(k) accounts; all other types of personally managed investments and savings

I need to reiterate that no one leg of this three-part retirement funding system was ever intended to be a sole retirement funding source for an individual or household. But, taken together as a triple stream of income, they were a very solid way to fund the retirement years. This approach was thought to allow Americans to create and maintain a more secure, multiple stream of income for financial security after retirement. The system was built to create a better standard of living in later years, in sharp contrast to the plight most Americans experienced during the World War years and the Great Depression early in the last century.

Until the three-legged system for retirement funding, most workers were on the job till their deaths – but that was no longer needed. We were living in the Golden Age and it reeled us in with its mandated and newly available voluntary options. We were lulled by the ease of it all. We let the system take over and take care of us. We now felt more carefree when we thought about our later years. These were approximately two short decades, but they represented the Golden Age of the U.S. retirement funding support system.

Things were so good, in fact, that we forgot to take care of ourselves with a personal "Plan B" or backup strategies of our own.

The Decline of the Retirement System (2000 - Present)

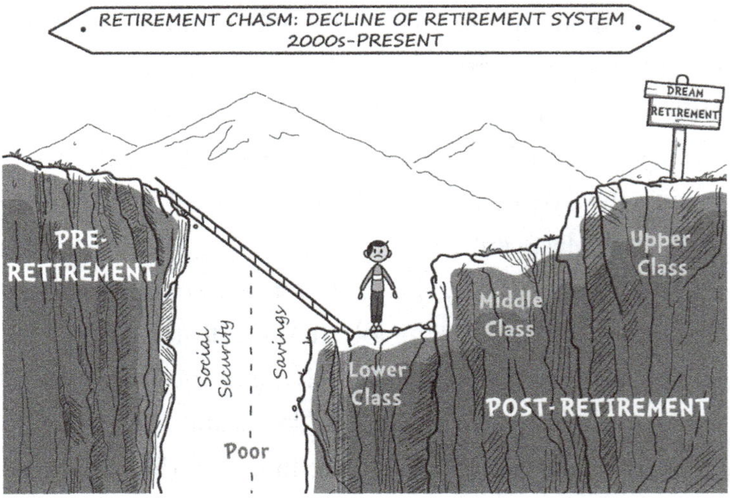

Americans entered the 21st century still confident in our system ... yet big changes were in store.

All three legs of our funding scheme were in for shocks. Just as our three-legged system was not created in a single day, neither has its decline happened all at once. That is the more dangerous aspect of the whole scenario: What creeps up on us can eventually shock us when we finally see it for what it is.

The decline of our retirement funding system has been slow and sporadic, much like its evolution.

The Nature of the Decline

So, what has been happening in this 21st century? Let's look at it from the perspective of each leg of the stool.

Pensions have gone away in massive numbers. By the opening salvo of the 21st century, and unbeknownst to the greater population, corporations were quietly closing down their pension schemes. The number of pension programs declined significantly, as corporations offering them decided to eliminate the legal liabilities and the direct and indirect administrative costs, and prioritize their own corporate profits instead.

While *public* sector pensions are still with us, the number of *private* sector pension plans continues to decline thanks to a complex regulatory environment and legal assault as government institutions make difficult decisions to avoid bankruptcy and other financial hardships.

- Pensions in the private sector have declined sharply: 35 percent of all private-sector workers had access to pensions in the early 1990s – the Golden Age of the system. The coverage in 2016 stood at only 15 percent, or about a sixth of all those private-sector workers.
- There were some 29,000 private-sector pension plans in 2006, and that number fell to around 22,000 by 2014.

The above numbers for the private sector are in big contrast to the public sector. Approximately 75 percent of public-sector workers are enjoying a pension plan – yet there are nearly as many private-sector workers (115 million) as public ones (133 million) in our country.

There is a clear imbalance. Unless you've been a public service employee, career military person or a union worker, chances are that today, in the 21st century, you don't have a pension. Indeed, only about 22 percent of you working outside those public sectors are likely to be a pension recipient in 2017.

Social Security is still there for us in this 21st century, you say? For now. Americans overall are very cynical about the longevity of the Social Security program. They are cynical as to how much of that money will come back to us. They fear politically driven future manipulations of the system. How much is Social Security really paying out to retirees?

- As of January 2017, the *average* payment to an American having worked full-time his entire life, was approximately $1,317/month.
- Any of you who started working later than average, worked extended part-time hours or suffered unemployment, may receive less than the average payment.
- An executive or other high earner, having earned high six figures in gross salary throughout that entire career, will only receive $2,600/month in

Social Security payments – that is the maximum allowed payment.

- By taking Social Security early (i.e., right at age 62), you lose potentially hundreds per month in payments for the rest of your life – but too many Americans are forced into age-62 enrollment just to make ends meet.

Payouts are perceived as remaining flat (although, truth be told, there was and still is *somewhat* of an adjustment for inflation), while the age/eligibility criteria increase. Congress has, more than once, increased the age at which you can start collecting on your years of contributions into the fund. This age change has effectively reduced and/or delayed individuals' ability to benefit from Social Security as an income source when it is sometimes desperately needed.

Our fear as a nation is that Congress will continue to reduce those benefits, put them out of reach due to later age requirements, or spend the fund entirely out of existence before most of us retire.

Voluntary Savings, as our third leg of this increasingly wobbly stool, has not expanded enough in this 21st century to compensate for the loss and decline of pension programs and Social Security. Indeed, there are two very good, and even hair-raising reasons for that decline:

1. In the opening months of this new century, the so-called dot-com bubble burst in the year 2000 and the financial markets collapsed in dramatic fashion. Then the events of 9/11/2001 and another market crash came right on its heels, and trillions in savings and profits from any account invested in the stock market were abruptly eliminated. Many future retirees counting on those sums were back to "no savings in the stock market account."
2. The 2007-08 financial and mortgage crisis and ensuing recession wiped out millions of households' real estate equity and employment. Some, barely caught up from the 2000 dot-com bubble and 9/11/2001 losses of financial wealth, saw their subsequent savings and real assets wiped out – again! Everyone who could fell back on cash savings ... and untold millions of us depleted those savings far, far too quickly. There is, today, simply very little money left to save and invest.

Some might circle back around and say, "Well, you have a job – just save more into your company's 401(k)." There are problems with this:

- More of you than ever lack access to employer-provided retirement plans such as 401(k)s. They are, alas, going the way of pensions.
- For those who do have access to 401(k)s, maximizing the benefits of those accounts has proven challenging for a multitude of reasons.

We have seen why we Americans as a population are not saving enough on our own into personal savings accounts or investments to offset this pair of losses to our retirement funds. We've been massively burned at least twice in a single decade in our attempts to do so. That means, taken individually, these voluntary savings accounts are not large enough at retirement time for any of us.

- For households nearing retirement with a 401(k) account, we are seeing a typical account balance of only about $100,000, and that includes assets that may have been rolled over into individual retirement accounts or IRAs.
- This translates to less than $400/month during retirement to add to our Social Security benefits.

Thus, our ability to develop Voluntary Personal Savings is currently in just as much jeopardy as the other two legs of our retirement funding stool.

The Rise and Fall of Our Retirement System

As you can see, the retirement funding system was not created all at once by a single act of Congress or a single agreement by corporate America. Another look at our history reminds us that the three legs of the system didn't all materialize in our workplace at once, but like the great Roman Empire, they rose slowly, at last coming together for us after decades of launching various programs. It did, indeed, enjoy quite a heyday in the late 20th century. Again, like the great Roman Empire, the decline of this system has not been materializing all at once either, but it is definitely underway.

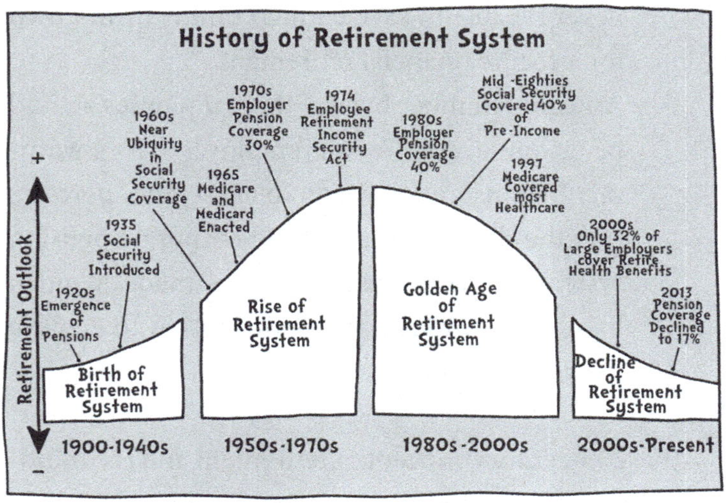

The Dream of Retirement

Today, we still have the not-so-old 20th-century concept of a pre-paid retirement embedded in our national psyche, yet we have also become very, very worried about our ability to achieve our collective dream of a financially secure, healthy retirement for all.

We can all see that our retirement funding support system is breaking down – fast:

- Over three fourths of Americans surveyed in 2015 are concerned that the economy and poor employment/earning rates will affect their abilities to save for retirement.

- 80 percent state that the average worker would never be able to save enough on his or her own for a secure financial retirement.
- An equal number believe that employees should be given access to an employer- or government-sponsored pension plan – and perceive that the disintegration of the corporate pension system in the United States has made it much harder for workers across the nation to achieve their retirement dreams.[13]

This 20th-century concept of retirement and the mindset about retirement security no longer works. Our so-called U.S. retirement system depended on a strong, vibrant retirement infrastructure (that stable three-legged stool of funding options) and that has been legislated away as the "costs to the nation" have been seen as too high. The foundations of growing our nest eggs now seem to have been dug into sand rather than cement. Major economic and financial sector failures in just these early years of the 21st century have likewise shown us how shaky our system really is.

The retirement funding system rose. It had its Golden Age. It is now in fast decline, falling into disuse and disrepair. And what is worse? There is no fix in sight.

What that means to all of us is that there is a big gap

– a chasm – between what we have for retirement and what we will need.

Dire Straits for Millions of Us

I chatted about retirement with many people in my parents' generation and with my peers as I prepared to write this book. I learned about the effects of the retirement-system breakdown. A number of them told me without hesitation that they had a few of the following:

- A corporate/union-managed pension
- A military/civil service (government-managed) pension
- A 401(k) account
- Personal savings
- Stock-option plans that they cashed in (or were still holding onto for various reasons)
- One or more personal investments like a condo or home, or other rental properties, or shares in an entrepreneurial business close to home
- A self-managed stock investment account

No single retiree had all these sources of retirement income, not by any means! And those who had just one or even two admitted that – pulled all together – it really wasn't enough cash. What was most disconcerting to me as I spoke with more individuals about this retirement funding decline was the number of 65-year-olds and up still working because they had to. The number of retirees who only had their Social Security money each month, alongside a very small personal savings account, was devastatingly high.

To make cash-strapped retirees' situations worse, all of those I spoke to have the federal medical insurance plan (Medicare or Medicaid), but very few have any supplementary health insurance to create a healthcare cushion. This is of concern given that health care is one of the largest expenses in our retirement budget. In 2017 the average couple was expected to spend an average of $275,000 for health care costs throughout retirement.[14]

Our legislators and corporate employers simply don't live in the real world or with the same circumstances as the rest of us. Because they don't, they are unwilling or unable to see what is going on – and they need to understand before they can take steps to improve the situation. The ability of Americans in the working-class and middle-class to save and financially prepare for retirement in save-as-we-work ways faces brick wall after brick wall. It leaves us all in a never-ending scramble to get along and get by … without ever feeling like we've gotten ahead.

Those in power to correct our retirement funding system are unconcerned with our plight because they either are unwilling or unable to acknowledge the looming catastrophe.

The Center for Retirement Research at Boston College finds that 52 percent of our households are at risk of not having *enough* to maintain their living standards in retirement. Added to that private research, the truth gets even more shocking:

- More than 38 million working-age households *don't have any* retirement account monies in employer-sponsored plans or IRAs, and likely very little in personal savings accounts at banks.
- GAO (Government Accountability Office) statistics show that many retirees and workers approaching retirement have limited financial resources for their later years, and confirm that about *half of households aged 55 and older have no* retirement savings at all.

Women are particularly challenged when it comes to preparing for and living through their retirement years in some comfort.

- Women are 80 percent more likely than men to be *impoverished* at age 65 and older.
- Women aged 75 to 79 were three times more likely to fall below the poverty level than males. This is due to multiple reasons including those we've mentioned, but also that females simply tend to outlive males. There are joined assets when married; when the husband dies, and his retirement

> monies expire, the widow's means are much reduced as a result – especially when spread over all the many, many years of her remaining life.[15]

In short, The Golden Age of our legacy retirement funding system is behind us. One by one, the legs of the stool have been broken. I have seen how we are really boxed in.

We are looking at a crumbling system and that affects millions of Americans who are on the brink of retiring. But it also affects millions more whose retirement is still 10 or more years in the future.

Women are 80 percent more likely than men to be impoverished at age 65 and older.

The system as it now exists no longer serves most of us and, essentially, no longer exists for massive numbers of American middle class workers, particularly those of us in the non-union, private sector.

The system is designed to keep you in a state of systematic, perpetual catch-up. How will *you* manage? Can you catch up? What kind of life in retirement will you have? By the time you finish reading this book, you will be able to answer those questions, and your answers will be better than you currently expect since up to this point you've been reading a historical background that may sound gloomy. Soon I will get to the Purchase Power Retirement Formula and the secret strategy for achieving the retirement of your dreams. But first, there's one more chapter with a dose of reality as a wake-up call.

CHAPTER 4:

DESPERATE MEASURES: FAILING TO ACHIEVE YOUR RETIREMENT SAVINGS GOALS

Most Americans preparing for retirement are … unprepared. I know I am repeating myself, but the statistics are shocking: The median savings for families whose wage earners are between 50 and 55 years old is only $8,000; those between 56 and 61 have just $17,000.

If current trends continue, the U.S. will face rates of poverty among senior citizens not seen since the Great Depression of the 1930s:

- Out of 18 million workers between the ages of 55 and 64 in 2012, more than four million will likely be poor, or near poverty level, by age 65.
- 2.6 million of that number are Americans who were considered middle class prior to retirement!
- It is estimated that by 2035, nearly 20 million retirees will be living in poverty or near-poverty, with that number rising to 25 million by 2050.[16]

I must say that, as a nation of wealth, circumstances are calamitous … and shameful.

We've seen the rise of the U.S. retirement-funding support system, and it is now clear that its Golden Age did not last nearly long enough for us. Its decline is upon us.

Compromise of Lifestyle and Quality of Life

Let's review, as we all move toward our retirement, how our quality of life is at risk:

- You who are older than 40, like me, are not likely to earn much more in your current job over the coming years. It is in your 40s that you reach your income peak. After 40, earnings will flatten or rapidly decline.
- Increased job insecurity after age 40 creates in-

come instability. Employers want your advanced skills and experience, but at a beginner's wage.

- Changing jobs voluntarily is risky after 40, even if you are head-hunted or hire an employment agency to help. You will need an airtight strategy of only taking the new job – fully negotiated, with contract signed – while you are still in the old one. Gaps in employment at any age, but especially after 40, are red flags to hiring managers.
- Financial institutions don't want you, the older investor, to be too aggressive with your investment portfolios, meaning your portfolio earns less. Advisors want you to increase conservative investing, moving out of the higher-risk, higher-return instruments in favor of the lower-earning, more stable ones. If you find yourself with only a few short years remaining to benefit from compounding earnings, this approach leaves you unable to build your retirement fund.
- Saving is very hard to begin at older ages if it has not been a habit before, especially if income stagnates or declines at the same time.

If you are approaching retirement, yet unprepared, you are not alone. To fix your dilemma, you have three options available:

1. Delay your retirement start-date
2. Never retire at all, and keep on working … and working
3. Downsize so that you simply need less cash during retirement

As you see in the image below, three different retirement doors are beckoning!

Let's look behind door #1, door #2 and door #3 (as they say on TV game shows).

Door #1: Delaying Retirement

You decide to put off retirement an extra year or longer. Those of you not really that far short of your savings goal might crunch the numbers and decide that earning a bit more and saving a lot more for a period of one, two or more years before leaving the workforce is all you need. But need it, you do!

When you earn that extra cash (assuming you do), investing it so that it earns more seems a logical next step. Yet, we have seen that investing is not for everyone. For many, it seems complex; understanding it is out of reach. Many of you are still feeling vulnerable from lost savings in past economic and financial downturns. Friends of my parents and many of my peers experienced a loss of their entire cash investment in the stock market either in the dot-com crash or the more recent crisis.

I, as many of you may have done, chose real estate for my preferred investment vehicle – and experienced the loss of that entire investment during the crash.

Add to that your wariness about how much time you have left for compounding or profit-building on your "new cash investments." Returns are not so juicy with fewer years between now and your retirement. So, you delay retirement and sock as much as possible into those accounts and investments.

Door #2: Forgo Retirement

This one is easy to explain, and it reminds me of the 2001 novel *Skipping Christmas* by John Grisham, which became a film called *Christmas with the Kranks*. The Kranks' big idea was to cancel Christmas … and (spoiler alert!) they failed utterly.

What is this option? You just work till you drop. You forgo retirement entirely. Sorry, but many, many people reaching their 60s just see no other way to make ends meet.

This option is available to all of us, you say? Think seriously about how feasible it is for you to continue working and earning, given your skills and your abilities, and given where you are working. It might be easier for self-employed individuals than for those working for a corporation or any business with a retirement age in place.

Add to those considerations this very important question: Do you possess the health, energy or will to keep on going in the workforce? This option demands that you:

- Keep working in your current job. How many of you will be forced out at a predetermined age from your salaried job? We tend to believe that we must all retire at a pre-determined legal age, but that is actually (in most cases) not so at all! Some companies still have guidelines and traditions about the retirement age, usually with 70 as the very highest cut-off. However, federal law has opened up most sectors by disallowing discriminatory or involuntary retirement for those over 70. Hidden in-company pressures may encourage or even give a hard push to your retirement, nonetheless. It's only active-duty military service and policing agencies (the FBI comes to mind) that stop at age 62 by law. And do not even consider leaving your current job at such an age in hopes of replacing it with another one: Age discrimination in the workplace, though illegal, is still very much our reality.

and/or

- Add an additional job or income-generating activity. The issue of "available time" is real. If you are still in a nine-to-five salaried position, weekday evening hours for other work are scarce. That leaves you with weekends to find some new, meaningful, income-producing activity. Yes, it is true that many Americans have a side gig or a side business or a moonlighting job. Is that available to us all? Probably not.

RETIREMENT CHASM: FORGO RETIREMENT

Door #3: Downsize for Retirement

There is a third option that millions of American choose, and I would argue that this one is available to us all, at least in principle: You decide to reduce your living expenses. You downsize.

You do this to achieve a cost of living in retirement that is within the income you think you will have then – less than today's income, in all cases. You imagine all sorts of changes you need to make to live more cheaply and spend less money from here on out.

It may mean selling your current high-cost apartment or home and leaving that higher-priced neighborhood you have been living in. You plan on moving to a smaller, cheaper residence in a more economical neighborhood. You might even do this if it means a longer commute to work each day in the meantime.

You think hard about this downsizing option. You strategically reduce expenses at least by retirement to make post-earning life more affordable. It means giving up one or more goods and services that you currently enjoy or need – but that cost you money. It means letting go of one or more beloved leisure activities or hobbies that are part of your current quality of life – because they cost you money rather than earn you money. You prioritize which ones to keep and which to stop paying for.

The "downside to downsizing," as it were, is that it can cost us money (when we are trying to save more) to move to that smaller residence. Beware of hidden costs that eat up your nest egg instead of replenishing it (closing costs, new insurance at higher rates, moving costs, etc.).

As I asked one of my friends recently: "Do you really need that two-story, five-bedroom, seven-TV house with a pool … now that all your kids are grown and gone and you are on your own?" Now is the time to ask yourself that type of harder question. (And as my friend ended up convincing himself, "Yeah, I do need it. I've worked hard to have this, to have all these possessions. Downsize? Ain't happenin'!"

We Americans just hate to give up our space, our possessions and stuff. We feel that downsizing means we will have a lower standard of living – that our quality of life goes down the tubes when we are obliged to downsize. Even in our society of abundance, we might need to look more dispassionately at this if we are to survive our retirement years.

Then, there is the emotional jolt of leaving it all and moving on after all these years. Especially when you think of the memories you've made over the years in that home.

Let's face it. Such changes are hard.

Side by side with the ultimate decision to downsize, which is voluntary, there are no doubt times when downsizing during your active years is imposed by circumstances <u>outside</u> your control. We saw this during the financial crisis of this early millennium, with so many homes going into foreclosure when owners lost their jobs. Because people had much less cash to spend, a spiral of business closings ensued.

Homes and possessions are a big deal to us in the United States, and that is why it is often a painful decision to downsize them. But, still, we think about it:

- 37 percent of homeowners would rather have a smaller than a larger home.
- 60 percent of homeowners whose homes are 2,000 sq. ft.^{2} or more would select a smaller home the next time around.
- Among baby boomers who are homeowners, 37 percent likewise say they will move at some point, with 42 percent of them saying they will select a smaller residence.
- The tiny-house movement has increased over 10 percent year-over-year in the past five years, though it is more often the younger ones among us making this downsizing choice, not retirees.[17]

Young or not so young, downsizing your lifestyle for financial reasons is not easy for everyone. None of us are happy to give up the quality of life we desire or have enjoyed our entire active lives.

• RETIREMENT CHASM: DOWNSIZE •

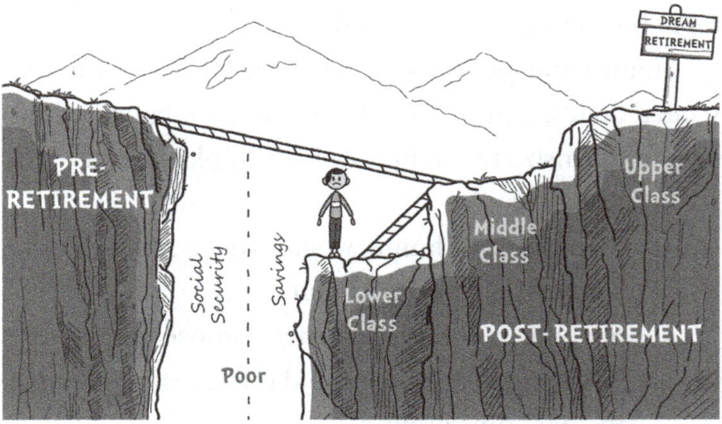

Failing to meet your retirement goal and having to consider alternative, less-ideal solutions for retirement is really tough. Many are led to believe that there are no other options for achieving a dream retirement, but there are.

In the next chapter, I will tell you about my personal journey to prepare for retirement and how I discovered purchase power. What I learned led me to reconsider how I viewed retirement – and I'm passing these learnings on to you.

Let's Review

About 75 percent of working Americans say they will work as long as possible and/or cut spending in retirement to be secure in their retirement years.

If you have not reached your desired financial goal but must prepare to retire, your options are to:

1. Delay retirement – to work longer or harder
2. Reduce living expenses – by downsizing your lifestyle; reducing amounts of cash you'll need
3. Forgo retirement – work forever or the "work till you drop" approach

These options require you, the future retiree, to sacrifice your standard of living today to adjust to your predicted budget constraints of tomorrow. None of these options is ideal, and I would implore you to keep an open mind about your real choices until you finish the book!

PART 2

Leverage Is a Solution for Achieving Your Dream Retirement

I have shown how most of us floated through the Fool's Paradise in our peak earning years of ages 20-40, and how we landed squarely in a Retirement Planning Paradox in our 40s and 50s. And then when our 60s roll around, we start thinking hard about our options for retirement – or if we ever can.

What to do when we've missed our savings goal and retirement is approaching? That is what the next chapters of this book are all about.

I promised you a solution to help you cross the Retirement Chasm. For now, let's call that solution "***Leverage***." Leverage comes in two important ways that I'll define and illustrate in the coming chapters.

CHAPTER 5:

WHAT IS PURCHASE POWER?

By your 20s, once out of school and in the workforce, you usually have some sort of vision for retirement, even if it's a vague concept ... even if it is too far away to be a top priority on your list of personal goals.

For me at that age, the goal was to retire by age 40, with one million dollars in savings.

For as long as I can remember, that was my main goal in life. I wanted to retire early and pursue my life's passions, and boy, was I relentless in achieving that goal!

I graduated in Computer Science from a top university in California and have worked for some of the best-known and respected technology companies in Silicon Valley. I am blessed to have earned a high six-figure income for my entire career.

My frustration? Being able to fully retire by 40 was still proving elusive. With a six-figure income, anyone reading this would probably ask, "So what was your problem, anyway?"

In 2003, I decided to turbocharge my retirement plan by jumping into the fast-growing real estate market with both feet, and my timing, as they say, couldn't have been better. I bought and sold numerous properties in and around Los Angeles, moving ever closer to my retirement goal with each transaction.

But in 2008 the real estate market crashed on me. On us all. And? That. Changed. Everything.

In a matter of months, my real estate portfolio had evaporated. I went from living in the Hollywood Hills amongst the stars … to renting a tiny room in a tiny home near the Hollywood Wax Museum of the stars.

My million-dollar retirement goal? It was by now a distant memory. I felt defeated, confused, hopeless. I had always achieved every goal I set in life, but not this one. To be honest, I hit rock bottom in lots of ways.

But then something interesting happened. My retired parents told me they were moving from Los Angeles to Las Vegas. They said it was a choice in order to lower their cost of living and improve their quality of life.

I was surprised by their decision, since I knew they really loved Los Angeles. However, once I visited their new home and community, I quickly understood their decision. I mean, I walked into a new, gorgeous six-bedroom, four-bathroom mini-mansion! It sat on the edge of a golf course in a private, gated community. They still socialized, made many new friends, dined out often, and most important? They were happier than ever before.

It struck me how different their lifestyle was compared to my godparents who retired at the same time, with a similar net worth. My godparents chose to remain in Los Angeles after retirement. They were forced to reduce their monthly budget and downsize, based on their fixed income in retirement and the higher cost of living associated with Los Angeles. They lived in a modest two-bedroom, one-bathroom bungalow home, in an even more modest neighborhood, and could barely afford the occasional meal at a decent restaurant. Even though they had similar income and savings levels as my parents, the sharp contrast in lifestyles and happiness really made an impression on me.

My Journey to Discovering Purchase Power

Remember me telling you that I spoke to several people while writing this book? Well, those conversations started around the time of these two very different retirements!

This observation of my parents and godparents led me to speak with a few other retirees and I quickly noticed a similar pattern. In general, people who retired to cities that offered a lower cost of living appeared to be more financially secure and satisfied with their lifestyles, while those who remained in their original city after retirement often had to downsize their lifestyles and inevitably were much less satisfied.

People who retire to cities with a lower cost of living appear to be more financially secure and satisfied with their lifestyles.

And with that, it hit me: The retirement lifestyle I desired never REALLY required a million dollars. If I leveraged (and there is the concept I promised to bring you) the benefits of purchasing power to lower my cost of living, I could reduce my retirement savings goal by as much as 75 percent, or in my case, to as little as $250,000 from $1M – and still maintain the lifestyle I wanted.

Needless to say, I was excited about this! I quickly put a plan together to begin researching various cities, but I hit a roadblock and became frustrated by the lack of information available to assist me in planning. There were no recognized experts to help or teach me what my options were. There was no advisor telling me to where I should consider relocating, or what risks and pitfalls I should avoid. I couldn't figure out how to proceed, and considered giving up.

But then I thought, why not become the expert myself? So instead of giving up, I started researching and interviewing countless retirees who took advantage of a better cost of living by relocating both inside and outside the U.S. I obsessed over their approaches, determined to understand when, where, why and how they pursued their relocation strategies. Eventually I knew more than most people in the industry, and seemingly on cue, people began to search for me – asking for my advice and recommendations. I felt confident, empowered and excited about my future again. I was finally in CONTROL of my retirement future.

As I began to share my knowledge with others experiencing major retirement-planning challenges, the positive impacts on their retirement plans were transformative. Their results were so compelling that I wrote this book to share my knowledge with everyone seeking to break free from their own retirement-planning struggles. Along the way I discovered that my real purpose in life was so much more than just retiring with a million dollars by age 40. My purpose became to help others in challenging financial situations achieve their dream retirements. I know you can, too.

Let's finally get into exactly what Purchase Power is and how it might benefit you! (And it's about much more than just moving to a less-expensive community.)

What Is Purchase Power?

Purchasing Power (or Purchase Power, as I prefer to call it) is the value of a currency, such as a dollar, in terms of the amount of goods or services it can buy.

Purchase Power can be understood by either analyzing inflation over a period of time, or comparatively analyzing the economies of two markets, such as two different cities. Let's take an inflation example first.

Price Inflation

Inflation increases the price of goods and services, and as a result decreases the amount of stuff you would be able to purchase with one dollar. Over time, inflation tends to increase, and with it the cost of goods and services also increases.

For example, if you took a dollar to a store in 1958, it would have been possible to buy a greater number of items than you could buy today. Most people know this means we've had price inflation. This means that one dollar would have greater purchase power in 1958 than it would this year.

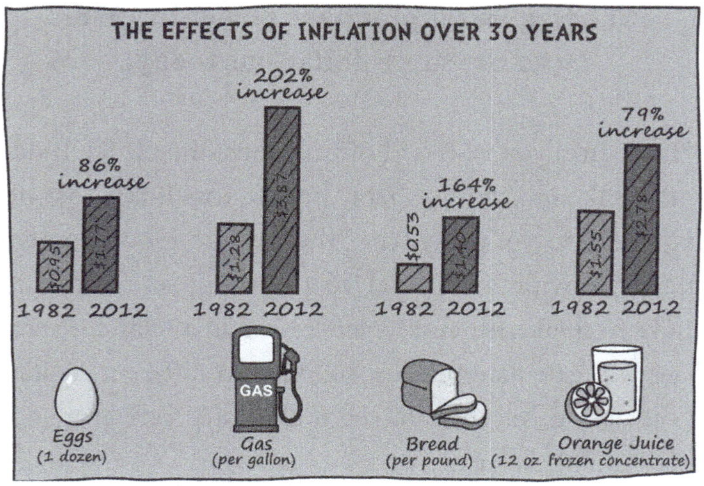

Cost of Living vs. Inflation Over Time

In the above diagram, the effects of inflation are captured over 30 years. For example, the cost of a gallon of gas increased 202 percent between 1982 and 2012, from $1.28 to $3.87. In that period, gas prices more than tripled ($1.28 x 3 = $3.84).

If you had a dollar in 1982, the value of your dollar or purchase power would have declined significantly over 30 years. In 2012, that same dollar only enabled you to purchase one-third of the gas you could have bought in 1982. If you were earning money and paying your own way back then, you know exactly what I'm talking about![18]

$1 had greater purchase power in 1958 than the same dollar has today.

I am sure you've heard of the Consumer Price Index (CPI). Like me, you probably believe that it is a cost-of-living index. Not really true. The American government doesn't provide an official cost-of-living index for us. Many nongovernmental agencies or financial corporations will calculate the cost of living in different regions of the nation, but the information doesn't come from our government, as a rule.

What is a "cost of living," then? It is simply the amount of money you need to maintain a certain level or quality of living in the place you reside.

We will include in that cost only your basic expenses – food, lodging/housing, healthcare expenses, transportation and taxes. Do you have other expenses? Of course, but the indices usually agree on those basic components. It is the short list of what absolutely everyone earning money spends it on. Taxes are included, for instance, since they vary from state to state, as well as from person to person. But a closer examination of each of these basic included expenses will show you that they all vary from place to place in the country.

Purchasing power depends on context. Cost of living is part of that context.

When you take your available cash – your fixed income as a retiree – to places around the country, you find that one of your dollars doesn't "get you" the same amount of goods and services in each place you visit. You are faced with the combined effect of purchasing power and cost of living.

A Tale of Two Cities

As noted earlier, purchase power and cost of living can also be understood by analyzing the economies of different markets or cities. For example, when analyzing different cities for their cost of living, purchase power can be clearly understood.

In Las Vegas, Nevada, the typical living cost is $2,500 per month. For all your basic expenses we listed above, that's the net amount of cash you'd need. However, in San Jose, California, living costs are over $4,500 per month. You need almost twice the cash to live in San Jose!

Granted, this difference is largely due to housing prices or costs. Here's how that happens:

Land in Las Vegas is plentiful (supply is high), so there's plenty of space at a reasonably low cost to build homes and apartment complexes. The tourism-driven economy virtually demands that salaries be low enough that services remain fairly cheap for tourists to buy. Low wages, in turn, lead to an overall housing supply that is less costly – if it didn't, owners or developers would find themselves with lots of vacancies on their hands.

Contrarily, there is a lack of vacant land available for building homes in San Jose (demand is higher than supply). The perpetually booming economy of the technology sector that the city benefits from, with its high salaries and wages, ultimately leads to high housing costs (when there is little supply of something and great demand, prices are pushed higher) and the related costs of living in the community associated with it.

Let me continue to travel further afield, with two different cities: San Diego, California, and Playa Del Carmen, Mexico.

Playa Del Carmen is an emerging city for international residents, and that includes Americans seeking first-class amenities for third-class prices. To maintain a standard of living in Playa Del Carmen equivalent to your $4,200 per month San Diego lifestyle would only cost you $1,250 per month.

You would only need to spend a quarter of the cash to live in Playa as to live in San Diego! What a huge difference! That's because, after considering prices of all services and goods you buy – haircuts, taxi rides, restaurant meals – the overall price level in Playa Del Carmen is much lower.

The greater the difference in cost of living between your current "home" city and your target city, the greater your purchase power.

In general, Mexico's low price level reflects the relative abundance of labor in Mexico. Because workers are in such great supply (in relation to job availability – remember "supply and demand"), their wages are very low. That, in turn, drives down the prices of many services provided by such workers. Such services represent a large share of overall consumption, and create an overall lower cost of living.

While I highlighted the relative advantages in two pairs of cities, the same principles apply to other lower- and middle-income cities in the U.S. and across the globe. This is not exclusive only to a U.S./Mexico comparison. Cities in the American Southeast, Midwest, and even Southwest offer significantly lower costs of living. Internationally, countries like Panama, Belize, Costa Rica, Malaysia, Spain and Thailand are just a few that offer significant cost savings over our example cities of San Diego or San Jose (and others more or as costly across the U.S.).

Locations such as these offer an undeniably high standard of living – giving you a bigger bang for your buck. You can "buy" a higher standard of living for fewer dollars than you are paying now at home. The greater the difference in cost of living between your current "home" city and your target city, the greater your purchase power.

Purchase Power relates directly to Cost of Living.

I take you back to my parents' and godparents' choices. My parents took their money, earned in a more expensive location, to a lower-cost location. Their purchasing power increased for retirement. My godparents likewise earned their money in a high-salary location but stayed in that location for retirement. Their purchasing power remained the same, but their budget in retirement shrank – they had less cash per month than when working, and still had the local high prices to pay from it.

If you move from a higher cost-of-living city to a lower one, you have greater purchasing power … more leverage … more bang for your buck.

Unfortunately, the opposite is true as well. If you move from a lower cost-of-living city to a higher one – from Playa Del Carmen to San Diego, for instance – you will have far less purchase power from your earnings/savings.

The consequences of moving to a city where you have less purchasing power can be financially devastating. If you insist on creating the same lifestyle, and spend, spend and spend more to create it – it will mean you run out of money faster. It's probably why we've never heard of anyone moving to New York City to retire!

Across the U.S., the cost of living can vary wildly, even among our largest cities. It is exactly the same in every country around the world. Simply by moving to a different region of the U.S., you can save tens of thousands of dollars per year – or even thousands per month, if you remember the San Diego/Playa Del Carmen example, and relocate to places as inexpensive as Latin America, the Caribbean or Southern Europe!

While some individuals who have lived in places like coastal California or the Northeast might not be inclined to relocate elsewhere just on stubborn principle, there are, in fact, real financial benefits to doing so, especially in retirement.

The ability to either save on expenses or improve your standard of living and quality of life on a limited budget, is a major advantage of moving to a lower-cost area – whether elsewhere in our United States or overseas.

• RETIREMENT CHASM: PURCHASE POWER •

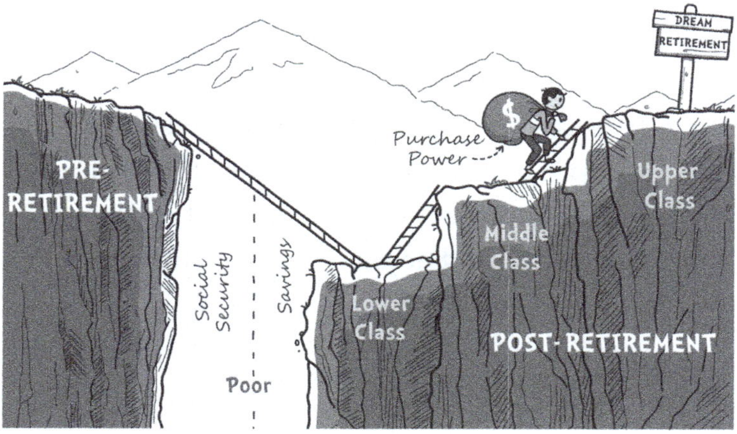

As the above image illustrates, and as I have described in prior examples, purchase power affords you upward mobility in retirement. It enables you to take what might be a lower-class or middle class lifestyle in your existing city and elevate yourself to a higher socio-economic class level. This is a very powerful concept if you are interested in achieving a particular standard of living or quality of life, regardless of what you have achieved financially.

Additional Benefits of Purchase Power

Hopefully you have a good understanding of how purchase power works and how it ties to the cost of living. I also hope you understand the concept of leverage – moving from a high-cost area to a low-cost area with your fixed amount of saved dollars or income to create your high-quality retirement.

Leverage is getting more bang for your buck.

Now let's examine the benefits of these three concepts called purchase power, cost of living and leverage. I'll show why you should account for all of them in your retirement strategy.

Purchase Power Amplifies Your Savings

Imagine this: You have a **Purchase Power Factory**, like my image above. You feed $100 of cash into one side and get $200 or $300 of value out of the other side.

Although, as I stated about my own million-dollar retirement goals, we can all increase the value of our savings by increasing our purchase power. Thus, my "need" for $1M quickly transformed into a "need" for only $250,000 – by using leverage.

Increasing your purchase power results in an increase in the value of your retirement income and/or savings to offer you greater financial leverage and control of your lifestyle.

Leverage means applying the cost of living and purchase power concepts so that your cash has more value. The number of dollars is unchanged. The value of your dollars skyrockets.

Living in a community during retirement with a lower cost of living than you are accustomed to has two outcomes:

1. You upgrade or improve your standard and quality of living with a budget similar to your pre-retirement one, enjoying even more of the goods and services you are used to or desire to access in retirement, or
2. You maintain your pre-retirement standard and quality of living, but you spend far fewer of your hard-earned, hard-saved dollars for those same goods and services – you get more bang for all your bucks, with no deprivation.

The additional savings benefit offers you much more flexibility in your retirement planning, enabling you to:

- Retire reasonably with a smaller portion of your otherwise required savings amount
- Experience a higher-quality lifestyle than you otherwise could
- Retire earlier based on your expected savings

Expand Your Borders

According to a recent Gallup poll, over 32 percent of Americans wish they could move out of state. And why not? Your ability to lower your cost of living increases dramatically as you expand your geographic boundaries of consideration. Meaning, if you live in a specific city in a particular area and decide to move to achieve a cost-of-living reduction, you will surely discover lower cost-of-living options in other towns or communities in the same county.[19]

Think about it: This is how suburbia got started! In-city housing was in such high demand, that prices sky-rocketed and families just couldn't make ends meet with so much cash going out the door for rent/mortgage. They moved outside the city for lower rent/mortgage costs.

What is more, these movers also maintained their previous lifestyles (or improved them if having a yard, cost-free parking, and so on, were items on their unfulfilled wish lists) and saved money doing so. Those movers were in control of their standard of living. While considering where to move, the families compared quality and availability of schools, grocery stores and other retailers and leisure amenities that were important to their quality of life. Then and only then would they move.

Who knows? Maybe moving outside the metropolis where they worked enabled these households to save more for retirement, too. If so, they had the option (the one I tried and failed to create for myself with my $1M goal and loss of investment in real estate) of retiring early.

For those of you residing in some of America's largest cities, can you think of cheaper neighborhoods than yours with similar characteristics within your metropolis? Probably! Can the rest of you name a cheaper place to live in your current county of residence? Chances are good that with a bit of head-scratching, research and conversation with locals, you can also do that. This concept is backed up by data as the following chart illustrates:

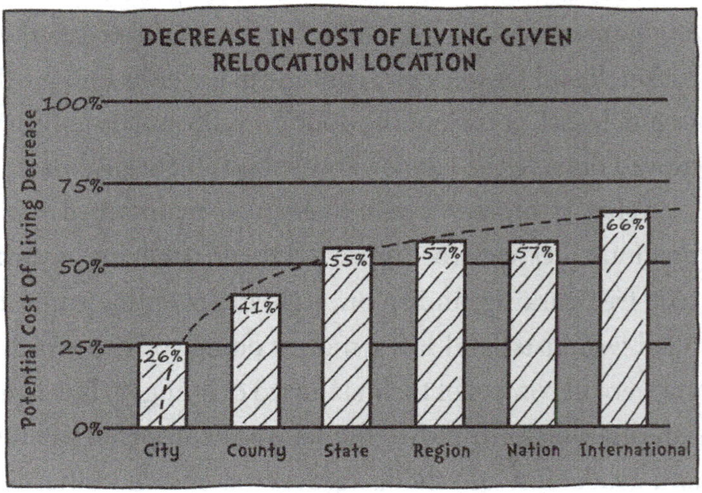

But expanding your geographic boundaries goes beyond just moving to the suburbs in your working years. Consider now such moves for your retirement years. The larger the geographic area you consider for your retirement relocation, the more savings you can achieve. So, as surely as you can save a little by relocating to a cheaper neighborhood in your current city (about 26 percent on average in most large cities), you can save even more of your dollars by relocating further afield but in your same county of residence (an average of 41 percent).

In summary, the above chart (created by the Retirocracy team) shows that:

- If you decide to relocate to another comparable neighborhood within your existing city, you are likely to reduce your cost of living by 26 percent – and not much more than that.
- By relocating within your existing county, you are likely to reduce your cost of living by as much as 41 percent.
- If you relocate somewhere within your existing state, you might reduce your cost of living by up to 55 percent.
- If you relocate within your region (e.g., Southwest, Northeast, Southeast, etc.), you'd experience a 57 percent savings.
- If you relocate nationally instead, you'd have the same 57 percent savings as relocating regionally.
- However, by relocating internationally, you jump to a 66 percent cost of living reduction!

This data proves that there is a compelling economic advantage to expanding the places to which we might consider relocating. However, Americans tend to do the opposite!

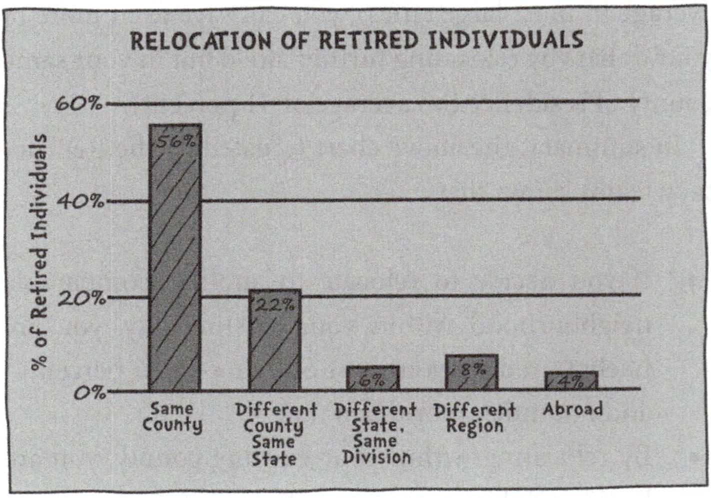

Based on the above chart, over 56 percent of retirees who relocated in 2016 did so within the same county. The next sizeable segment was 22 percent of retirees relocating within the same state. Most moves are resolutely "local." More than twice as many people move within their county as move outside it.[20]

More than twice as many people move within their county as move outside it.

Based on these clear financial advantages, I'd expect an increasing number of retirees to move farther from their same city or county in the future to experience the standard of living and quality of life they want.

The farther you consider moving from your existing city, the more likely you are to discover the higher standard of living you desire ... and at a (much) lower cost.

And yet ...

Most relocations tend to be local and thus do not enjoy a great cost-of-living reduction ... or increases in purchase power.

Well, that is the data from surveys taken by the experts. Despite the monetary benefits (savings in your cost of living), most relocations tend to be local and thus do not enjoy a great cost-of-living reduction … or increases in purchase power.

The bottom line for the majority: People don't typically move with the goals of maximizing costs of living and standards or quality of living in mind!

Your new bottom line: Move with the largest cost-of-living savings and purchase power increases in mind!

But, let's not be hasty, since one of the next stories shows why some (at least) of the movers within the same city/county might have made a good financial choice.

Getting Personal

In general, your cost of living – in relation to the amount of dollars you have – determines your purchasing power. However, your purchasing power is rarely static.

Let's get down to specific examples. Here are two stories from conversations with my peers and retirees.

Lois, a friend of mine from Los Angeles, thought she was suffering from the nation's highest rents and living costs … until her friend Beth from Boston arrived to visit and opened up the cost-of-living conversation. In reaction to how much typical rents were in L.A., Beth exclaimed, "Oh my, it's really cheap in L.A. compared to Boston!"

Friends of my parents had always lived and worked in the Upper Midwest – Chicago and Minneapolis. They retired to Florida after many visits there as vacationers. Why? The cost of living in Florida was observably less because of many nonexistent or greatly reduced local costs – compared to what they'd known and paid in Minnesota and Chicagoland (the heating bill not the least of them) during their entire working lives. They had repeatedly experienced how cheap it was to dine out or purchase services like car washes or lawn work, or to rent or buy a home in Florida – compared to their northerly homes.

What Beth from Boston and the Chicago couple were referring to was their perceived (in Beth's case) and actual (in the Chicago couple's case) purchasing power in the new location.

Let's look at the statistical data (and by now you know I love the data). I also chatted with Eric. He currently lives in Santa Monica, California, where his total cost of living expenses are $5,400/month – that's his "must-spend" to continue living there. He is open to moving anywhere in the country for his retirement, and to base his choice on the cost-of-living data I've shown you so far. But he has not yet decided where to relocate.

Eric and I sat with the data I'm talking about, but only as applied to the city of Santa Monica. Watch what we discovered for Eric, and you'll see more clearly why Beth was delighted at Los Angeles and our Midwesterners decided to choose Florida.

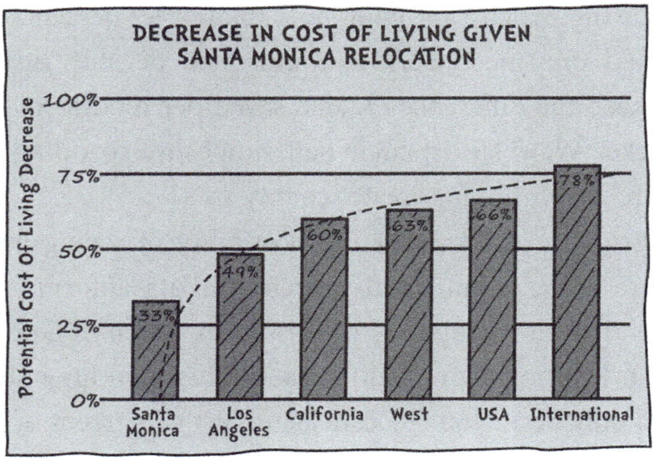

Eric lives in a neighborhood with the median cost of living for Santa Monica. This means there are an equal number of neighborhoods in town both more and less expensive than his current one. If he relocates to one of the lower-cost neighborhoods in Santa Monica, he could likely achieve a maximum cost-of-living savings of 33 percent or be spending $3,618/month rather than his current $5,400/month. He could keep the difference of $1,782 in his pocket! (As you see, our percentages change from city to city; while the national average was a 26 percent savings, in this city it is 33 percent).

If Eric instead relocated to one of the comparable lower-cost-of-living areas (Venice Beach, Hermosa, Marina Del Rey, Redondo Beach, etc.) in the county of Los Angeles, of which Santa Monica is a part, he could likely reduce his cost of living by an additional 16 percent – reducing his cost of living by a total of 49 percent. He would only need $2,754/month. He'd be able, again, to keep the difference ($2,646 saved per month) in his pocket. Wow! Nearly cut in half, simply by expanding his search to within his greater county area.

Eric is excited about the possibility of saving even more, so we expanded his search to all of California. He sees that his savings has now risen to a total of 60 percent. He can stay in California and his monthly outlay will only be $2,160. He can spend just 40 percent of his Santa Monica budget by living in a comparable beach community elsewhere in the state of California.

He discovered that there was little additional cost savings to moving out of the state or to another location in the Western Region. Nor were there any greater savings to be had for him anywhere nationwide (remember that this applies to Eric, for this example of Santa Monica – your analysis will give different results). In all, Eric has a potential gain of 60 percent by relocating to a comparable city.

However, Eric and I were not quite done. He was shocked when he looked at moving overseas (an additional option that he was open to considering). He really had no expectation that it could gain him more than the 60 percent he'd already gained. Yet that type of move offered another percentage gain, and boosted him to a total savings of 78 percent over his Santa Monica costs and expenses. He'd need to spend approximately $1,188/month … a cost savings of $4,212 per month over his current cost of living! Again, please note: This additional gain is not to be had in just any foreign location but is based on a select few international cities that he (and you, soon) looked at with comparable beach town characteristics to Santa Monica and in relation to his current Santa Monica costs.

By relocating with the amount of cash and income he knew he'd have, he would only be spending 22¢ on the dollar to achieve his same lifestyle!

There is a moral to Beth's, Lois's and Eric's stories (and it will apply to your own story), and it is this:

The larger the territory under consideration for relocation, the more you can increase your Purchase Power through a reduction in your cost of living.

Move wisely ... with the largest cost-of-living savings and Purchase Power increase in mind!

You also see that Eric, if he did not wish to leave his home state, would still have enjoyed a 60 percent cost-of-living reduction just by moving elsewhere in the state. Sixty percent might be all he, or you for that matter, needs to ensure a high-quality retirement (and I know some of you are surely picking yourself up after the shock of such savings potential). Also note that the smaller the geographic boundary Eric considered, the harder it would be for him to identify a comparable city with similar characteristics as Santa Monica in his desired price range, so by expanding his search to cities nationally or even internationally, he increased his chances of finding a city that satisfied both his cost-of-living AND lifestyle choices.

So, to recap, here are the key advantages for broadening or expanding your geographic territory for relocation:

- You will be more likely to find a community that meets your top lifestyle requirements.

- All costs of living are not equal, so more choices give you more chances of identifying a match with your unique criteria.
- Some locations that save you big money may not offer better amenities or services, resources, safety, communities, healthcare, etc., than others. So, the more locations under consideration, the better your chances of finding a fit.

Relocating to Get Ahead Is Nothing New

Now that I've demonstrated through real stories and data how advantageous relocation can be, you may have begun to recall friends or family who have relocated … but you may wonder if they used data to make their choices. My guess is that they really haven't. That doesn't mean you cannot.

Relocation just means moving from one place to another. We know this. Between 2012 and 2013, about 36 million Americans moved to a new home. That represents about one in every eight or nine people.

The U.S. Census Bureau tracks such relocations in our society – and why we make them.

In the 2012-2013 survey, the Bureau found that Americans moved for these reasons:

- Housing needs
  - A new or better residence
  - A newer or cheaper residence
  - A better or safer neighborhood
  - More space for a growing family
  - Smaller space for empty-nesters
- Family reasons
  - Moving due to divorce
  - Caring for ill family member living in different location
  - Starting one's own household
- Job and employment
  - Relocating to be near a new career opportunity, especially for those earning $50,000+ in that job
- Financial downturns, whatever the cause

Many of my research conversations with people revolved, as I showed above, around their own reasons and strategies for relocation. During our active working lives, relocations are made for many other, and quite specific, reasons:

- A parental decision might be to relocate to a good school district, when that simply means moving from one suburb to another in the same metropolitan area.
- A decision to relocate to a different state might allow career advancement because there is a major employer there seeking your skills.
- Some relocations for young adults are to attend a distant college, get away from the parents, or to follow a boyfriend or girlfriend.
- Conversely, we move to be closer to family members, for whatever reason and at all ages.

We are a mobile society and we relocate, it seems, quite readily. None of the above reasons for moving shock us. They are part of the fiber of our society and our way of living.

There is one other reason to relocate that is by now obvious to you. Relocation is also done to create greater purchasing power in retirement. That means consciously moving from a high cost-of-living location to a lower cost-of-living location. This, of course, assumes that all things are equal. When you have the same number of dollars in the high-cost location as in the low-cost location, your purchasing power is increased. For retirees with a fixed or limited income, this creates leverage for a quality retirement.

CHAPTER 6:

THE PURCHASE POWER MOVEMENT

We've just seen reasons Americans give for moving – whether to a new neighborhood or across the country – and they vary from "for the kids' schooling" to "got a great new job" to "safer neighborhood." None of these reasons are shocking or uncommon. We are a mobile people and the reasons for our mobility are clearly understood by us all.

Domestic moves happen by the millions every year in our vast nation. As the map below shows, Florida and the Southeastern coast, southern Nevada and Arizona are the most popular domestic states where retirees move. Yes, we'd love to retire to Hawaii, but it is the most expensive state in the Union! There's not enough purchase power there for most of us. We have many other attractive areas in our nation that offer **greater purchase power** to us.

By now, you should also be considering not only other U.S. regions, but also any number of overseas locations when you are looking to **maximize your retirement lifestyle**.

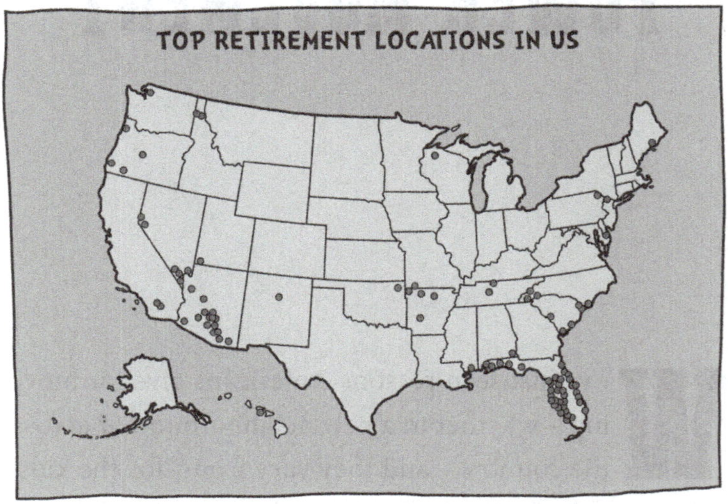

Overseas Relocations

When we consider moving for retirement purposes, our reasons for relocating or moving (the ones I mentioned in the previous chapter) change somewhat, and not surprisingly. Not just for retirement, but at any time in our active lives, we have told researchers[21] that:

- 35 percent of us would consider leaving the U.S. to live in another country.

- 55 percent of the millennial generation would also consider doing so.[22]

The top three cited reasons for this type of overseas relocation?

36 percent – Better quality of life
33 percent – Lower cost of living
31 percent – New experiences

The top three most important benefits or gains native-born Americans who move out of the U.S. hope to find/have found – at any age?

58 percent – More affordable healthcare than in the U.S.
51 percent – Lower taxes than in the U.S.
48 percent – An improved education system

There is more! We are counting a never-before-seen number of U.S. citizens who are – additional to what I have already presented – discontented with the "way things are" here at home. They are fed up with our politics and the wide-ranging shenanigans of our elected/appointed political representatives. Fed up with the inadequate responses from them and our governmental institutions. Fed up, too, with the behind-the-scenes taxation, economic and financial market rigging that play against the average American just trying to get ahead.

Who are these disgruntled Americans who are emigrating, or seriously considering doing so? The people next door! They are business owners from your neighborhood, school teachers, skilled knowledge workers or high technology workers. They are folks whose values are not being comforted completely enough. They are also just folks … seeking to stretch their retirement dollars elsewhere.

Terms such as migration, emigration and expatriation don't tell the whole story about Americans' desire for overseas adventures or ventures. This is partly because travel is cheap. Moving from the U.S. to someplace like the country of Panama is no harder than moving from the U.S. West coast to the U.S. East coast. Digital connections – internet, email, Skype and so on – allow us to stay in touch as before.

Emigration Is Just Relocation

As I write this book in early 2018, immigration – both legal and illegal – into the United States (and into the member nations of the European Union as well) has remained in the headlines. Accept new immigrants or reject them? But what about the flipside of that immigration coin? What about American emigration, or the flow of Americans out of the U.S.A.? How many Americans (beyond domestic moving alone) have emigrated – relocated – overseas?

That is indeed the $64,000 question, since the U.S. government has difficulties estimating with any reliability how many of us live temporarily or permanently outside the United States. In fact, the U.S. is the only developed nation that cannot count its expatriate citizens. The U.S. Census Bureau counts only those of us living in the 50 states and U.S. territories at the time of the census count. Our airlines industry probably has a more accurate number, by the State Department's own claim, of the numbers of us leaving the country than our government does. This said, in 2016, the U.S. State Department estimated that 9 million citizens were living overseas, either temporarily or permanently (and this estimate does not include overseas military personnel). Consider that more than 1 million American citizens live in Mexico alone.

Without a doubt, there are millions of us overseas at any given time as vacationers making short trips, as relocated Americans staying anywhere from one month to 11 months a year in a foreign country, and as permanent emigres living in another nation.

To our long list of reasons we relocate, then, we must add:[23]

- Economic reasons related to cost of living and purchasing power
- Retirement from an active working life (aging), and new freedom to be mobile
- Seeking adventure, such as in overseas relo-

cations or in moving to a radically different climate or cultural life from our U.S. community

- Returning to our country of ancestry/birth
- Pursuit of religious faith or religious activities, such as missionary work, or volunteering for causes we believe in
- Departure due to political reasons

The Relocation Movement

I hate to admit it, but none of what I am telling you about relocation is new to mankind. From the first horse or camel that someone tamed to carry a rider, from the first ships that man learned to navigate – man has been relocating!

Curiosity is a shared human trait, and the most curious among our ancestors were the world travelers. There is, I think, a bigger and more global shift going on, and it's happening for adults of all ages – not just retirees in their 60s and beyond. The global trend is to think of world travel as so much easier now than ever before because of the existence of:

- Instant digital access to our money
- Free or dirt-cheap digital communications with our loved ones

- Real-time research and all kinds of information at our fingertips thanks to the internet
- Low-cost airfares that make travel by airplane a popular and efficient form of transportation
- The so-called rise of the "digital nomad" with the ability to work from anywhere on the planet with an internet connection

Previously ignored areas (by those of us from the developed Western world) of Latin America, Asia, Europe and the African continent are now politically open to us. These regions are likewise more easily economically available since they've gone digital. That means we can access our money digitally from almost everywhere in these nations by now, too. Our American "can-do" attitude and spirit can now safely take us anywhere on the planet our hearts desire – in retirement, too.

Retirement and Relocation Personas

I'd like to regroup what I've been presenting to you – the reasons people relocate, and where – by sharing the **personalities** of relocators that we can easily identify. You might, naturally, identify with one of these personalities at any age.

These personalities, or **personas**, can be found across the retiree population, without a doubt. Please notice that not all personas, whatever the age of relocation, relocate for financial reasons. Not at all, as you will soon see. There are **nine persona groups** according to my observations and research. Which one (or ones) are you?

Adventure Persona – seeking new adventures and discoveries, or to reinvent one's self through travel, whether at home and/or abroad.

Affluence Persona – looking to create a more affluent, prosperous experience, or upgraded lifestyle than the current one.

Digital Nomad Persona – moving overseas while pursuing or managing an income-producing business venture; the typical choice is to live in a lower cost-of-living city than before. This reduces the amount of revenue your burgeoning venture must produce early on. It's critical to pursue ventures that are easily managed remotely or over the internet.

Return to Roots Persona – returning to a country of origin (first-generation U.S. immigrants) or of heritage (long-time U.S. citizens); this persona may also return to a domestic hometown which is in a region they previously left for various reasons that might include working/earning.

Better Quality of Life Persona – moving to a more prosperous area of the country/world that supports a higher standard of health, comfort, and happiness. This might include surrounding oneself with a more beautiful (urban/natural) or enriching environment.

Better Standard of Living Persona – seeking a bigger bang for fixed-income retirement bucks.

Early Retirement Persona – opt to relocate to a lower cost-of-living location in order to effectively retire sooner, or leave the traditional work environment to continue working on a part-time basis with a better work-life balance.

Health and Wellness Persona – this group is moving into places with affordable, high quality medical care availability for particular needs; moving into locations where health/wellness is more of a cultural or lifestyle priority; seeking healthier climates conducive to creating/maintaining health.

Investment Persona – this group seeks destinations that offer business opportunities with potentially significant ROI (return on invested money); ventures often involve real estate or tourism, amongst other industries.

Other Relocation Considerations

With all the reasons for relocation, we still have more! Perhaps – if you have not yet recognized yourself – you will see other considerations that make relocation the logical choice.

Relocation need not be forever. It need not be "once and done." We are, after all, a mobile people! There are many choices and options for us. Consider that relocation might take you …

- **To a location that supports a part-time or seasonal relocation experience**: Many Americans live "six months here, six months there" while others move and stay put. You can even travel back and forth based on seasonality or weather conditions.
- **U.S. Southwest vs. Southeast vs. Midwest**: Our continental U.S. offers such a vast range of climates, cultures, sights, sounds, environments, activities and costs of living that making a list is hard (but I am, as you will see more clearly, still trying to do so!).
- **Domestic vs. international relocation**: Passports are easy to come by. Travel satisfies so many searches and relocation personas!
- **Latin America vs. Asia vs. Europe**: Again, satisfying your curiosity about unknown continents, their people, languages, traditions and cultures; the different foods and low cost of living might take you to an exotic continent.

Top Non-Financial Benefits of Relocation

As reflected in the list of personas, we don't relocate for financial reasons alone. Here are more reasons:

- **Reinvention**
  When you move to a city where no one knows you, you can start over again!
- **Challenge**
  When you don't yet know "how things are done," you can challenge yourself to learn and grow further.
- **Fulfillment**
  We create a monotony of life when we are in our daily working routine. Look back with no regrets; look back with many moments to feel proud of. Some of my fondest personal memories relate to my various travel experiences.
- **Curiosity**
  There are new things you want to see and share and – let's face it – not all of them are in the neighborhood you live in!
- **Open mind and heart**
  You have skills, knowledge and talents that you just might have an opportunity to share ... if you relocate and immerse

yourself in a different environment, with different folks.

- **Discovery of yourself**

  It may sound like a cliché, but travel and living in a new city are the ultimate experiences for helping you find yourself. Nothing beats the survival instinct that kicks in when you wander off a beaten trail or lose yourself among strangers in a vast city, state or country.

- **A Personal Sense of Accomplishment**

  When you look back on the time you spent in another place, you will be able to look back with fond memories and feel proud of the fact that you were able to deal with the stress that came with moving to another city.

You will notice how much you have achieved in your new city. You will have made new friends and found a good place to live. You will have come to understand and adjust to a new culture. You will have grown as a person and that experience is incredibly valuable and truly unique!

Taking the Guesswork Out of the Equation

Many retirees do not choose where to relocate based on informed calculations. None of the retirees I spoke to could say to me with any certainty, "We're moving from a $3,000-per-month cost-of-living area to a $1,500-per-month area."

I'd like to reiterate my goals in writing this book and launching the PPRF solution:

- To help you relocate for a great retirement and to do so by *design* and by *choice*.
- To offer you a clear, logical rationale for your decision to relocate for retirement.
- To make it easier for you to identify relocation opportunities.
- To help you know what you are getting into ... before getting into it.
- And most importantly, to help you achieve your dream retirement.

This includes **knowing that your quality of life or standard of living will be equal to or greater than your current one and definitely NOT less.**

Yes, there are many reasons to relocate, and I have tried to present them all so that every one of you reading this might grab onto something you identify with. But as we near retirement, what may drive many of us to relocate, by default or design, is our frustration at not being on track in achieving our retirement financial goals. We should also stubbornly resist those other unsatisfactory options:

- Delaying our retirement
- Canceling our retirement
- Reducing our standard of living during retirement

Not being on track to financially achieve our retirement goal offers a huge motivation to consider relocation as a solution.

If you are determined to start your next chapter of life – retirement – on time, committed to retiring on YOUR own terms, and desire a way to make your retirement vision a reality – I encourage you to join the Retirement Relocation Movement.

CHAPTER 7:

WOULD RELOCATION ACTUALLY WORK FOR YOU?

Domestic or international relocation can provide a wide range of comfortable solutions for you – all of which contribute to a rich life in your retirement years. But I am going to play my own devil's advocate now, because by this point, you are probably kicking up some objections to my whole "relocate and things will be great" approach to retirement. I get that. So, let's look at a few challenges that your mind might be hashing over.

There are many misconceptions that relate to relocating locally, nationally or internationally. The first is that "everyone can do it." **Yes**, everyone can. But **no**, not everyone should.

Here are just two instances that illustrate why going overseas – or simply relocating to a vastly different region of the U.S. – is not for everyone:

1. If you have trouble interacting with people who just do things differently (and in your opinion, not as well or not as efficiently as you do), you may not enjoy the adaptations necessary for living in a city much different from your present one. If **"different from me"** has a scary meaning, you'll relocate domestically (in my opinion) more comfortably than overseas.
2. If you are a **Type A** personality, you might not enjoy the apparent "no hurry" lifestyle of many foreign cultures or of some regions even in the U.S. You may get impatient just trying to figure out how things work or how to make them work faster *for you.* Frustration rather than joy will be your daily lot. Your choices may be limited exclusively to the most-developed or metropolitan parts of the U.S. and the world, and even then, you may face challenges.

I witnessed a combination of these two barriers when I spoke to a Santa Barbara, California, couple who desperately wanted to own/live on and work a farm. They found their heart's desire in the lower cost of living of Arkansas. But this couple just couldn't figure out how to fit in, get things done or be taken seriously as "city folk who've gone rural." They were beginning to see that the culture shock – even in our own country – can be quite real. They knew others who had successfully done it, which is why they did it, too. But by speaking with them, I saw that they were not the "adaptable" kind of folks. Things had to be their way or not at all. Thus, this was not the best retirement choice.

That is why my Retirement Persona list in the prior chapter is so important. You can see that not only your retirement persona, but the fullness of your own personality might make you cross some types of relocation off of your solutions list. I hope to convince you that other types of relocation will suit you to perfection!

Common Objections

Let's examine reasons (excuses, false beliefs, misconceptions – call them what you will) that may lead you to say relocation might not make sense for you. Keep in mind that I am not trying to change your mind or convince you that your objection is just a tiny detail and you can overcome it. Sometimes just being aware of what your mind is saying wakes you up to the fact that it is … just your mind! You may not have all the facts yet. Stay open and stay with me, as you ask yourself if you are throwing obstacles in your way that don't need to be there.

Aversion to Change

This is just resistance to new or different people and environments. Aversion to change, or resistance to change, is quite human, so don't beat yourself up too much about that. But – don't cave in to it, either!

Uncertainty or confusion about how things are done can trigger anxiety and even paralyze some people. But it is all about how you respond. As the saying goes, "It is not what happens to you but how you handle it which tells others who you are." Sure, familiar faces and surroundings give you a sense of security. But there are other advantages to reaching outside the known, outside the comfort zone you've built around you. One of them is that you get to step up and test yourself. We push our kids to do it, and as time rolls by, we forget to do it ourselves. Walk your talk!

Impatience

Impatience with slower-paced environments might be a big deal to some types of personalities. Those whom we call Type As or dominant "get it done" types of individuals might struggle in slower-paced environments – and there are many of these relaxed places in our own nation, as well as abroad.

Big-city East Coasters are seen by the more laid-back Midwesterner or Californian as "hyper" – thinking fast, talking fast and moving quickly. In European cities, you'll experience a slow-paced lunch or dinner in a restaurant, and if you are a Type A, you'll be frustrated that everything isn't brought out at our same U.S. "fast" food pace. There are advantages to such slower paces: People around you are less aggressive, impatient or rude. They are willing to take the time and effort to really hear you. They might even walk with you to the store you seek to make sure you are comfortable getting there (instead of just giving you verbal directions). Humans love to connect! Enjoy that.

Frustration

If you are the kind of thinker who struggles with or gets frustrated with sudden obstacles thrown on your path or with puzzles to figure out, there's no way around it: Moving to a new place will offer its fair share of challenges for you. This will be true whether you move elsewhere in the U.S. or go abroad.

The more different or foreign the city from your current location, the greater the challenge you will experience. Figuring out where to shop or eat is usually the first challenge. Making yourself understood, finding new friends and buying a car in your new location are going to be confusing. Again, there are advantages to this: Look on the bright side and look at how much you learned that first day out in your new hometown. We don't learn everything we need to know from a guide book, a video or even other travelers. We – all of us – really learn best by doing. So learn! Take your time, because the clock is an illusion (you are in retirement now, remember?).

Sounds Interesting, But Still Not Sure

If this all sounds interesting to you, great! However, if your very next words are, "But I don't know *if* it would work for me," then let me give you some food for thought.

"Not sure it will work for me because ________."

If you are tempted to fill in that blank with something like:

- I've never been much of a traveler
- I can't imagine leaving my friends or family
- It's only for major risk-takers
- I am not very well organized
- It's only for loners and nomads
- I don't speak other languages
- I don't make friends easily …

Do you eat the exact same meal day after day? Probably not. Do you perform the exact same tasks at the exact same hour every day? Probably not. Life is about movement and trying new things – mixing it up because it gets you out of your boring routine. Life is about trying or learning something new (and letting it go if you don't like it). Every day of your life, you are doing something new – and not all of those new things will be keepers.

You're not a risk taker? My mom always told me when she'd serve a new food or a new dish at our dinner table,

"Taste it once. That's the only way to know if you like it." I say the same to you: You will not know if relocation works for you unless you try it. Tasting that new vegetable is a tiny risk in comparison to finding a brand-new, healthy food you actually like to eat! Life is like that.

You are not one of those nomads or loners or adventurers? Who said you had to be? Relocation doesn't mean going out into the wild and pitching a tent and living off the land. It does not mean trekking the highlands for the rest of your days. You'll choose a location that comforts your sense of people, environment, climate and activities. You can live in a crowded, friendly place with lots of group activities (if that is your thing) much more easily than out in the wild!

If you don't yet speak another language, move to a city where people speak English, or better yet, learn a new language! Have a fun time with your new neighbors' children – that is how one of my own friends learned French right in Paris. She spoke the same two phrases every morning to the same waiter at the corner café; she struck up a maternal conversation with her apartment house's children, who began to wave and run over when they saw her. Take it slow. Learn that foreign language like you learned the one you speak now: by imitating, by taking your time, and through fun!

Leaving Friends and Family

For some this can be difficult, and family and friends might not understand why anyone might consider leaving your current city, but there are ways to make relocation work.

With the evolution of technology, friends and family are only a video chat, email or phone call away. These days you can live halfway across the world and feel like you're actually in the same city as your loved ones.

Move to a city they would enjoy visiting. If you pick a city you'd enjoy, there's a good chance your friends and relatives would enjoy visiting regularly as well. Make relocating fun and exciting for others.

Keep in mind that relocating doesn't have to be forever. Every day you are living in a lower cost of living location, you are saving more money than you would otherwise. So if all else fails, you can always bite the bullet and move back if you become homesick or miss your family or friends and still come out financially ahead! So, don't deny yourself the opportunity to experience the retirement of your dreams by eliminating relocation as a viable option. Be open-minded and willing to give it a try.

Culture Shocks

You are saying, "Hmmm, things in other parts of the U.S. or overseas are just too different. I don't know the culture or language and I'll get screwed over if I misunderstand anything." Or, "I'll feel anxious about the living situations (food, transportation, social customs and ___________)."

We have change and shock right here in our own hometown if we are honest. People from our own cultural upbringing surprise and shock us every day (and if you doubt that, listen to the nightly news, just once, for proof). Again, I'd like to remind you how much your maturity and experience figure in here: It is not what happens to you, but how you <u>handle</u> it which makes all the difference. First, you might find that new cultural difference fascinating, and love it. Then, you'll grow familiar with it since it surrounds you daily. Then, you'll accept it as your new normal (and after all, what is normal?). In the end, it will be part of your landscape. When friends or family come to visit you in your new home, you'll laugh at their shock at that tradition! And be able to comfort them with all its history and explanations …

While change can be challenging, it is not what happens to you, but how you <u>handle</u> it which makes all the difference.

Will We Be Safe There?

One thing we all notice when we hear the news broadcast is that every day, every minute, every hour, people are committing crime or being victims of it, and the world is a highly dangerous place. That is – *if you believe what you hear.* I personally know people who have never, in decades of life and living, witnessed or been close to violence. I personally know parents who raised their children in neighborhoods reputed to be highly crime-ridden, yet they and their children never saw a glimpse of it. Crime, violence, danger? They exist. I am not denying that. But why focus on it? Focus instead on finding and going to places that are best known for safe streets. Look at relocating to communities where people look out for each other, are open to mutual inter-aid and support. Those places are out there – all over the planet. Choose one!

Can I Pull It Off?

Are you now thinking, "Relocation sounds good – it is an attractive option to me – but I don't know *if I could successfully pull it off*"?

You are experiencing an emotional tug. Your heart says, "I might feel isolated from loved ones – homesick. What if I cannot make new friends where I go? I will be lonesome." That feeling of separation has nothing to do with distance, really. Many of us live within a two-hour drive of most of our relatives, yet how often do we make the drive and sit together? Once a year? Twice? You can just as easily hop on a plane if that is your frequency of face-time. And don't forget about video messaging services such as Skype, FaceTime and so on.

Some of you are thinking about the financial aspect of a relocation when you ask, "Can I pull this off financially? Will I have the lifestyle I desire over there?" Part of that worry can be remedied by doing the homework on your new location. That is a big piece of the PPRF – the Purchase Power Retirement Formula shows you the costs of the new location in relation to the amenities and quality of life that you get for that money. You can, in other words, fully plan before relocating. You can write up your budget and financial plan for your new home. Set up local bank accounts; learn about the tax picture, etc.

Fear of Failing

You might be thinking, "I'm too old for a big change. Can't teach this middle-aged dog new tricks. I'll just grin and bear it right where I am. No relocating for me, no sir!" Too old? Then why are you reading this book? I think you have – with that one thought – revealed that you really do want to succeed. Success is all about the right information and enough information to make a solid decision. The PPRF gives you all the information you need, based on what you seek in retirement.

Overwhelmed

You might say, "Yes, that's all well and good, but I've never been a planner. There are too many new factors to consider. I feel lost before I've left!"

Think back about when you left for college outside your hometown, or when you moved to a new house in a new city or neighborhood. You surely didn't know everything about that new place but did a bit of basic research and just made the move. Now, with maturity and an understanding of your preferred lifestyle in retirement, you know exactly what questions to ask. What is more, the answers are out there for free, and those that are not – well, you can buy a plane ticket and go see for yourself. A sort of reconnaissance trip.

PPRF invites you to identify your lifestyle criteria. These include your amount of savings and your monthly retirement income, and your core needs in the location (weather, safety, climate, healthcare, distance from friends and family, local culture and other activities, and so on). From that information, the PPRF moves you to research eligible cities – only those cities that satisfy all your stated criteria and budget.

It is true – for better or for worse – that we adopt our beliefs at such a young age that we are not very critical of their truth or falsehood. That is why, in this next section, I will ask you to do a bit of personal research on a region of the U.S. or the overseas cities or regions that you have no direct and personal experience in. If you can travel there, great! Nothing changes our minds faster than going to a place we had preconceived notions about and seeing for ourselves that what we thought to be true "just ain't so.'"

If you feel, you might still say to me, "Well, this all sounds interesting, but I'm still not sure. Will I be safe there? Will I feel a culture shock that is far too strong? This is still sort of overwhelming." You may just be impatient to develop a solution *right now* but feel overwhelmed by the thinking and research to be done.

Don't worry! You might regret it if you move. You might regret it if you don't. Knowledge is power, and there are aspects of moving that you should investigate to determine if relocating to a specific city makes sense. Let's see in the next chapter how the PPRF makes this quite easy for you![24]

CHAPTER 8:

PPRF EXPLAINED

By now you may be wondering, "What **exactly** is the Purchase Power Retirement Formula?" And even more importantly, "Will it work **for me**?"

What is the PPRF? The ***Purchase Power Retirement Formula*** is a system for identifying your retirement needs and successfully *discovering, evaluating, validating and relocating* to the best city for you, either domestically or internationally, based on your retirement goals.

The idea of relocation is simple yet can quickly become complicated.

It's simple: The concept of relocating to lower your cost of living so your dream retirement can happen is a straightforward notion.

It's complicated: There is a mountain of details to consider in order to successfully choose the right place for that relocation.

Once you have decided to consider the concept of relocation in retirement, lots of options open up for you. But lots of questions also arise, beyond the ones in the previous chapter, such as:

- Which cities meet my affordability requirements, even with my small savings and cash income?
- How hard is it to be a permanent resident there, or to come and go?
- What are my year-round weather/climate options?
- Which amenities must I have access to, and where are they available?
- Would I prefer living near the beach, mountains or a vibrant cosmopolitan city?
- Does a small-town lifestyle resonate with me, or am I resolutely a big-city person?
- What city meets most of my needs yet is less than a two-hour air flight from my current city?
- And many more!

While the opportunity offered by relocation is powerful and can be life-changing, figuring out how to actually get it off the ground can mean doing a lot of research. You want to find that one city that meets all your needs and desires, BUT:

- There are over 380,000 cities in the world.
- There are over 19,000 cities in the U.S. alone.

Where do you start? Finding the perfect location/city seems like finding that proverbial needle in a haystack. There are, indeed, a lot of details to consider to ensure that you create your ideal experience – financially, environmentally, medically, culturally, transportation-wise and so on. And by the way, the process is the same whether you choose a city life or a country life for retirement.

It isn't enough to just move to the first place that comes to mind. Nor is it enough to move somewhere because you already know someone living there.

This decision is far too important to your retirement standard of living, quality of life and ultimately your happiness. The PPRF helps you approach relocation in an organized way, thoughtfully and pragmatically.

When I personally discovered the power of relocation as a tool for achieving my dream retirement, I was enamored by the possibilities offered by this simple concept. However, I dove in to the research and quickly became frustrated and overwhelmed by the challenges of planning and executing a retirement-relocation strategy. I knew there had to be a better way. Unfortunately, that better approach required knowledge and expertise that I certainly didn't have at the time. I took it upon myself to research and study people who had relocated for retirement purposes – both successful and unsuccessful relocations, domestic and international moves. I noticed

a pattern of steps that were taken by the most successful relocators (as I like to call them). Conversely, I saw what research or steps were not taken by those whose relocations "failed" them.

As a result of my research and sharing the PPRF, I am taking the burden and confusion of much of the research off of your shoulders.

What about that other important question, "Will relocation work **for me** in **my** retirement?" To find out, you simply dive in to the PPRF, following along step by step. Remember, the PPRF is a system for identifying your retirement needs and discovering, evaluating, validating and relocating to *the **best** city for you, either domestically or internationally.*

The PPRF respects your retirement goals! But what is more, it helps you achieve them.

- PPRF will work for anyone who wants to achieve a dream retirement.
- It can be applied in any retirement savings situation – whether you have saved a little or a lot.
- It works regardless of what your specific retirement goals might be.
- People apply the PPRF with the goal of retiring early, experiencing a great retirement or creating a much more affluent lifestyle for themselves.

I've been observing, interviewing and tracking retirees making the relocation decision for several years now, and I started sharing my expertise with future retirees soon after my extended research. I have witnessed first-hand how the formula has helped people, in very difficult circumstances, to rethink and redefine their retirement experience in ways that they hardly could have imagined before.

So, without further ado, let's jump in to the **Purchase Power Retirement Formula**. The PPRF is a system comprised of a series of required activities or steps designed to ensure you effectively identify your financial needs and relocation options based on your personal preferences. It also includes a proprietary model to help you quickly determine which destinations in our curated list of cities would help you maintain your standard of living on a lower-than-expected retirement savings. The model will also help you identify cities that offer you the ability to upgrade your lifestyle.

NOTE: The PPRF guides and templates for each of the steps referenced in this book are available on the Retirocracy website. Please refer to the website to use the complete set of tools that help you successfully execute your search and relocation. Find those tools on www.retirocracy.com/pprf/tools

The steps of the PPRF help you evaluate as many locations as possible – and reduce that long list of domestic and international cities to a small, manageable set of locations (less than five is ideal) that meet your stated goals and criteria.

Even if you're skeptical about relocating and still don't think it's the best option for you, there's no harm in opening the tool and going through the steps. The results may surprise (and excite!) you, and at the very least they will give you options to consider. Give it a try.

The steps represent a practical approach to vetting your top locations in relation to your needs, goals and criteria. You take an organized approach, which gradually filters down to a short list of destination cities for you, even as it builds the amount of valuable, decision-supporting knowledge you collect.

The steps help you take the direct, hands-on actions to confirm that one or more locations are appropriate for you. The PPRF takes you all the way to establishing local networks of people (other relocated individuals but also local professionals) in the chosen community – ensuring your seamless, low-risk, well-informed transition into that community and into your affordable, high-quality retirement lifestyle.

Here is a quick look at the steps the **PPRF** takes you through:

1. Imagine and define your ideal retirement lifestyle.
2. Define your financial needs to support that dream lifestyle.
3. Determine your expected retirement savings amount.

4. Identify eligible cities meeting your financial needs.
5. Identify cities meeting the criteria of your primary retirement persona(s).
6. Identify cities meeting your lifestyle and quality-of-life preferences.
7. Arrive at your short list of eligible cities.
8. Perform the remote research on those cities.
9. Tour short-listed cities.
10. Connect with both relocators and locals (relocation experts and others) in those communities.
11. Take another, extended, trip or two to the destination city or cities.
12. Finalize your decision – choose a city.
13. Move and begin settling in.

The PPRF process – along with the templates and filtering tools found on the Retirocracy website – sounds reasonable. The steps are intentionally simple to perform. Each step builds on the prior one, allowing you to build a readiness for relocation. When you get to the final step, you will know that you have cast the widest net possible out to cities in the U.S. and the world – and chosen the top one for your goals, needs and stated criteria. The PPRF has saved you valuable time, but also offered peace of mind by minimizing any risks associated with relocating.

Implementing the PPRF steps can go as fast or as

slowly as you'd like. I've seen people take as long as a year or more, and others as quickly as a couple of months. If you prefer a faster approach that requires less effort and manual steps, I would encourage you to utilize the online tools at Retirocracy.com/pprf/tools, designed to fast-track discovering the best cities for you. Otherwise, if you are comfortable with a longer, more manual approach to identifying your needs, researching the best cities, and touring and validating those cities, than the basic approach outlined below will be sufficient.

Choosing between the manual vs. online PPRF process will dictate your pace and effort.

Let's move into more detail on each of the above steps, to show you the depth of analysis and preparation the PPRF achieves for your retirement relocation – reducing your costs of living, increasing your purchase power and helping you experience a high quality of retirement living.

#1 Dream Retirement Lifestyle

Sit and just imagine your <u>dream</u> retirement. You should assume that money is no object. It is important to envision your ideal post-retirement lifestyle regardless of cost or your existing budget. If you are retiring as a couple, sit together and dream out loud. Have you ever stopped to think about what you really want your lifestyle to look like? It's important to have a clear understanding of what type of lifestyle will make you happy when you retire. Vague, poorly defined dreams are too abstract to act on – especially when you may have several more years before you retire. Doing this imagining is one of the most important steps when applying the PPRF to your retirement.

Envisioning your dream retirement is one of the most important and difficult steps when applying PPRF.

The following kinds of questions (and their answers) are just a start, but will help you focus so that you can create a concrete plan for retirement:

- Is it your goal to simply maintain your existing lifestyle?
- Or do you aim to improve your quality of life during retirement with more affluence, amenities or experiences that you have denied yourself till now?
- Has it been your dream to live near the ocean or in the mountains?
- How old would you like to (will you) be when you retire?
- Are you interested in working part-time or even full-time upon retirement?
- Are you interested in spending more time on a hobby?

- Would you like to contribute locally (volunteer); if yes, what types of activities or areas of interest would you seek?
- Do you want to travel?
- Do you want to reserve time to visit with friends or family?
- If you'd like to live on the beach, how populated will the ideal beach community be?
- Should the waves be calm and carefree, or large and wild?
- Should the beach offer water sports, fishing, or just great swimming?

As you open your imagination to all the possibilities for retirement, you should also be aware of the fears or (false) assumptions that limit you. For example, do you fear never being able to afford to retire? Are you afraid that you will be bored once you stop working? Do you fear that wherever else you move, you won't have the services or amenities you want?

It is important to envision your ideal post-retirement lifestyle, regardless of cost or your existing budget.

Build a clear, vivid, unconstrained picture of what you want retirement to look like. The sky's the limit. There should be no limitations placed on your vision! The point is to really paint a complete picture in your mind –

on each aspect of that dream retirement. Such questions help you fully visualize the lifestyle and experience you desire.

It's also important to be excited about what you come up with – don't create a ho-hum retirement! If you aren't energized by your dream, you are less likely to pursue it, and you probably haven't dreamed big enough … so go back to the drawing board.

Tip: Consider using a vision board to help you imagine your dream lifestyle. You can find templates and links to digital vision boards at www.retirocracy.com/pprf/tools

#2 Financial Needs to Support That Dream Lifestyle

Dreams cost money, or so the saying goes. Now that you have a clear understanding of what you want your dream retirement lifestyle to look like, it's time to sharpen those pencils and power up your calculator to understand what it will cost.

This is a vital step to understanding where you might land *without the PPRF*! Like Eric of Santa Monica, whose cost of living in his working years was quite high in relation to much of the U.S., you need to know what your dream lifestyle *would* cost you, all things being equal. So bear with me! Like Eric, you'll be finding solutions that are lower in cost yet support your higher-quality dream retirement, too – as you work your way through the steps of the PPRF.

For now, *assume* you will need a lot more cash than you think. Then plan to add even more to that high number. This isn't to depress you; you simply need a realistic understanding of your expected expenses. No one wants to retire and go broke; you can retire to ensure financial stability through *planning for it.*

As you crunch those numbers, keep the following strategies in mind:

- Base your expenses on where you have always (before PPRF) imagined/planned on living in your retirement.
- Estimate conservatively: *Don't* plan on spending significantly *less* than you do today. Be realistic and cautious in your budget estimates.

When estimating the expense of your desired retirement, keep in mind that there is no right way to calculate how much money you will need during retirement. There are a lot of variables to consider.

A quick way to estimate it is to take your current take-home pay and deduct expenses that you aren't planning to experience in retirement. For example, if you have a mortgage payment now but you expect it to be cut in half or fully paid off by the time you retire, write that lower expense into this dream-retirement calculation. If you have transportation costs related to work, but much of them will stop after you retire, remove those excess gas, parking and vehicle maintenance expenses from your list.

Conversely, it is also important to add new expenses to your budget that may not exist today but will in retirement. This is vital if your dream is to scale-up your existing lifestyle with additional benefits. For example, account for upgrades to your existing lifestyle, such as living near the beach (costlier). Add cash to your medical budget, as most people require more healthcare in their later years and lots of that might be out of pocket.

Now again, some of you are protesting! You may be grousing at me, saying, "What's the point of including expenses based on my ideal retirement? I'm not even sure I could afford to even maintain my current lifestyle, let alone a better one during retirement!?"

Stay with me on this! There will be plenty of opportunity as we continue applying PPRF to align your lifestyle with the *realities* of your *actual* retirement budget. For now, it's important to get a clear, realistic understanding of how much your dream retirement would cost you right where you are. This estimation exercise gives you a quick way to cost out your dream retirement.

However, for an even more accurate assessment of this cost, you will need to create an actual budget. Be honest and realistic. Make a written list now of all monthly costs. As you get a handle on your retirement expenses, be sure to account for the following:

a) Any inflation growth between now and when you retire. Add 2 percent per year to each item on your budget.
b) Did you include taxes and insurance of all kinds?
c) Include medical expenses (e.g.: healthcare premiums such as Medicare Part B, a generous amount for out-of-pocket treatment costs, long-term care insurance premiums, etc.).
d) The little expenses add up, so put them in the budget, too (breakfast at a diner three times a week; monthly movie or concert tickets; treats like pastry and coffee on your way home from an appointment; etc.)

If you are unable or unprepared to create a detailed estimate of your retirement expenses, you can also use a simplified approach for now that involves reducing your existing budget by 5-20 percent based on how similar (or not) you expect your future retirement experience to be from your current lifestyle, and using the result as your target retirement budget. For example, if I earn $75,000 per year and desire a similarly high-quality lifestyle, I would only reduce my current salary by 5 percent or $3,750. This means I should target a retirement budget of $71,250 per year to maintain my overall standard of living and quality of life.

Please do not pass out. If your dream-retirement budget has you shouting at me, "NO WAY can we do this! You're NUTS!" – relax! I am on my way to demonstrating that you can indeed afford that dream retirement – and *where* you could live to enjoy it without breaking the bank. Keep reading how the PPRF takes you there. That vision of your dream retirement is achievable with the power of the PPRF guiding you.

Note: You will find a template and tools for estimating expenses for your dream retirement at www.retirocracy.com/pprf/tools

#3 Determining the Retirement Income Gap

In this step, you will determine what your retirement income gap is in order to identify what specific cities are likely to enable you to still successfully achieve your dream retirement, based on your projected income shortfall.

To define your retirement savings gap, confirm:

1) What your retirement savings should be.
2) What your retirement savings is on track to become, based on your current savings.

This is an important step because PPRF will help you discover locations that offer you the cost-of-living target you would need to remain in line with your standard of living and quality-of-life retirement standards. Here you are <u>not</u> dreaming and imagining – but being realistic!

How much cash will *really* be coming in during your retirement years?

People just don't do this! (And what is worse, they don't do it in relation to their **costs** of living in retirement). Do the basic math now. Write it all up. Start with what your income and savings should be.

Determine your savings gap by subtracting your expected retirement savings amount from your desired amount.

While seldom discussed broadly, it is well known within Financial Services circles that your post-retirement savings gap is likely to correlate with your savings gap today. Meaning if you are currently 25 percent behind on your savings goal, it is reasonable to expect your retirement savings to be about 25 percent below your goal once you retire as well.

This is because savings and spending habits are pretty much set for most of us, and while it's not impossible to break those habits, it does take either luck or a unique individual to make the necessary adjustments to close whatever savings gap might have existed prior to retirement.

For the purposes of your planning, let's apply this conservative principle to your retirement savings projection.

RETIREMENT SAVINGS TARGETS BY AGE

Annual Salary / Target by Age	$50K	$75K	$100K	$150K	$200K	$250K	$300K
35	$15K(.3x)	$90K(1x)	$150K(2x)	$315K(2x)	$520K(3x)	$750K(3x)	$960K(3.2x)
40	$40K(.8x)	$143K(2x)	$230K(2x)	$465K(3x)	$740K(4x)	$1M(4x)	$1.3M(4x)
45	$75K(2x)	$210K(3x)	$330K(3x)	$480K(3x)	$980K(5x)	$1.4M(5x)	$1.7M(6x)
50	$120K(2x)	$293K(4x)	$450K(5x)	$840K(6x)	$1.3M(6x)	$1.8M(7x)	$2.2M(7x)
55	$170K(3x)	$390K(5x)	$590K(6x)	$1M(7x)	$1.6M(8x)	$2.3M(9x)	$2.8M(9x)
60	$225K(5x)	$510K(7x)	$750K(8x)	$1.4M(9x)	$2M(10x)	$2.8M(11x)	$3.5M(12x)
65	$305K(6x)	$660K(9x)	$980K(10x)	$1.8M(12x)	$2.7M(13x)	$3.6M(14x)	$4.4M(15x)

1. First use the Retirement Savings by Age chart in Step #2 to determine how much you should have currently saved, based on your age and salary.
2. Next divide what you have saved so far for retirement from what the Savings by Age table recommends you should have saved right now. For example, if you have $100,000 saved for retirement and the savings table advises that you have $330,000 by your current age, then you'd calculate $100,000 ÷ $330,000 = .30 = 30%.
3. The final step is to subtract your percentage by 100 percent. Or 100% – 30% = 70%.

In this example, if you only saved $100,000, but should have saved $330,000, you'd be on track to miss your retirement savings goal by **70 percent**. Again, the calculation for the previous example was:

1 – ($100,000 / $330,000) = .70 or 70%

Now calculate the percentage of your retirement gap, based on the above example. The specific formula is as follows:

1 – (present retirement savings amount / retirement savings target) = retirement savings gap %

This calculation for savings or income gap is a simple method for defining your savings gap, based on your retirement savings amount. It does not consider any other potential sources of retirement income you may have that might help lower your income gap further, such as Social Security and pensions. For an even more accurate assessment, consider the following questions:

a) What is your Social Security payout likely to be? Look at the statement you get in the mail or go online.
b) What is the expected amount of your pension?
c) Add the net passive income you may receive (either monthly or quarterly) – include dividend income, royalties, rental income from real estate, and so on.
d) Do you plan to liquidate any assets, such as selling your primary home, your car, etc.? How will that factor into your retirement savings goal?

Will you work part- or full-time after retirement? Be sure to account for that income in your planning.

These are the types of **periodic retirement income** you already know. Write them up as an annual amount you expect to receive at the time of retirement, then add it up so you can see the annual income it all represents. Once you have determined the annual income, you must translate that amount into an equivalent present-day savings amount.

Including social security to determine your present-day savings total can be a bit tricky. In this case you'll need to work your way back by first determining your projected monthly income, and then translating it into a present day savings based on your expected annual income, and your target withdrawal rate.

For example: Based on your current contribution, if you are expecting $335 per month in monthly Social Security income once you reach age 63 and you expect to withdraw 3% of your savings per year, the present-day savings amount is calculated as follows:

$$\$335 \times 12 \text{ months} / 3\% = \$134{,}000$$

Or your $335 per month in Social Security income is equivalent to about $134,000 in present-day lump-sum retirement savings. This assumes a common 3 percent annual withdrawal rate from your savings.

If we combine your Social Security amount with your retirement savings, that total savings amount jumps from $100,000 to the approximate equivalent of $234,000. Which makes your savings gap 29 percent instead of the previously estimated 70 percent. The following calculation was performed to determine 29 percent:

$$1 - (\$234{,}000 / \$330{,}000) = .29 \text{ or } 29\%$$

Determining your savings gap is an important measure, since as we've discussed, the older you become, the harder it is to change the trajectory of your retirement savings result. Said another away, if your savings gap was 29 percent at age 44, like the above example, you are likely to reach retirement age in your mid-60s with an approximate 29 percent savings deficit.

There's another reason determining your present savings gap is an important measure: It relates directly to your purchase power factor.

Your purchase power relates directly to your present savings gap.

Are you on track to achieve your recommended retirement savings goal? We've seen, in the early chapters of this book, that most people are not even close! Don't worry – here is where the ***Purchase Power Retirement Formula*** kicks in to guide you.

To reiterate, the goal of this PPRF step is to:

- Determine if you are on track with your lump-sum cash savings goal for retirement, or not.
- If not on track, determine the percentage shortfall.
- Use that percentage shortfall to determine your **purchase power factor**.

Your purchase power factor will represent the level of purchase power you will need in a different city, given your retirement savings gap and desire to meet or exceed your pre-retirement standard of living and lifestyle goals.

Let's find your **purchase power factor**. If you haven't already done so, compute your savings gap, based on the formula discussed earlier.

Let's say you have only saved **25 percent** of what experts recommend saving at your age. We have already discussed the obstacles to reaching 100 percent of your goal. Is there enough money for the dream retirement you imagined in Step 1 and costed in Steps 2? Or is there a gap? Your savings gap is your ***purchase power factor***, which will range from 0 percent to 100 percent.

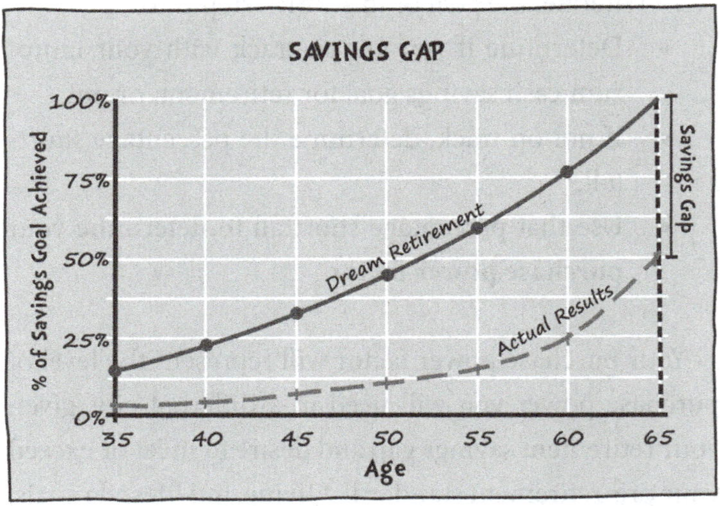

Example:

You previously determined that achieving your dream retirement (all things being equal) would require **$1.65 million** in lump-sum cash savings. This would give you **$49,500** per year to pay your living costs (using the 3-percent-per-annum rule of thumb that assumes you will withdraw at most 3 percent annually from your savings balance). This lump sum included any expected pension and Social Security income.

Let's also admit, though, that your retirement savings is, in fact, on track ONLY for **$800,000** – or **48 percent** of your $1.65 million savings target.

That means you are going to be able to spend only **$24,000** per year (again, this is the 3-percent rule).

Based on your current rate of savings and the

amount you expect to save, you have only saved **48 percent** of your retirement-goal amount. That gives you a **purchase power factor of 52** (or 100 x (100% – 48%) = 52). The formula is as follows:

Purchase Power Factor = 100 x (100% – your expected retirement savings-to-goal %)

Do that math for yourself now for your own dream retirement and your current savings trajectory. Even if you are on track for less than 10 percent of your retirement savings goal, write that down. Honesty, please.

Based on PPRF, there will be a cost-effective solution for you wherever you are in your savings goal!

Understanding where your savings level will end up is immensely helpful during the next stage of planning.

Remember your **purchase power factor**. You will apply it in the next step.

NOTE: You will find a template and tools for forecasting your retirement savings and income and determining your savings gap at www.retirocracy.com/pprf/tools

#4 Eligible Cities Meeting Your Financial Needs

Now that you have confirmed your projected retirement savings and expected shortfall, it's time to identify cities that **match your financial reality**. These will be U.S. and/or foreign cities. I would suggest you cast your net as wide as possible and include all cities ... you can fine-tune later if you change your mind. For now, be open to all of what the PPRF recommends to you.

As part of PPRF, the next step is to apply your purchase power factor to the Cost-of-Living Matrix Chart below. This chart has placed a curated list of top cities in the U.S. and around the world into segments (groups) from 1–10 based on their cost-of-living value. A classification of **1** shows cities with the **lowest** cost of living, while a classification of **10** shows cities with the **highest** cost of living.

The chart below illustrates the intersection between two different city segments representing 1) the city you currently reside in (left vertical column: Origin City) and 2) the city you might consider as your retirement city (horizontal axis: Destination City). The bottom half of the Cost-of-Living Matrix chart is blank, since those intersections would mean potentially relocating from a less expensive city to a more expensive city, which should be avoided if you have a savings gap yet desire an optimal retirement lifestyle.

The point of this chart is to easily identify which destination cities you should consider based on your current city of residence, and your projected retirement savings gap or purchase power factor.

NOTE: In the Resources section of this book, you will find a sample list of cities to demonstrate the PPRF's Cost-of-Living Matrix chart. For a complete list of international and domestic cities and their classifications, view the cost-of-living chart on the Retirocracy website: www.retirocracy.com/pprf/tools

Steps:

1) Go to the sample City Cost-of-Living table in the Resources section of this book and identify the city that you **currently reside in**. Be sure to note the segment level (e.g., 1–10) associated with the city you select. If you don't see your specific city, select the closest listed city with the most similar living costs as yours.
2) Now review the Cost-of-Living Matrix below and locate the bracket value of your present city in the **origin city section** (vertical left column), and look for the purchase power factor (the percentage numbers in the chart) that matches the one you determined in the previous PPRF step (#3 – Determining Retirement Income Gap).

COST OF LIVING MATRIX

		Destination City									
		1	2	3	4	5	6	7	8	9	10
Origin City	1	0%	90%	80%	69%	59%	48%	37%	27%	16%	5%
	2		0%	89%	77%	65%	53%	41%	29%	18%	6%
	3			0%	87%	73%	60%	47%	33%	20%	7%
	4				0%	85%	69%	54%	38%	23%	8%
	5					0%	82%	64%	45%	27%	9%
	6						0%	78%	55%	33%	11%
	7							0%	71%	43%	14%
	8								0%	60%	20%
	9									0%	33%
	10										0%

a) You may not see your exact purchase power factor percentage value for your Orgin City. If not, round up to the nearest value in your row. For example, if you live in a city with a cost-of-living value of 5, go to the origin city column and look for **5.** For the purposes of this example, assume your purchase power factor, based on your retirement savings gap, is **69 percent** – this means you are on track to miss your retirement savings goal by 69 percent. Now look horizontally across row **5** and you will find that 69 percent doesn't exist in the chart for that row. The closest values are **82 percent** and **64 percent.** You should round up to **82 percent**, since it is the next highest value in row 5. Eighty-two percent intersects with Segment 6 in the **destination city** axis. This means that you can consider relocating to any city in the City Cost-of-Living table that has a bracket value of **6**.

Consider cities with a higher purchase power factor when you want to upgrade or improve your lifestyle.

b) Now based on the segment(s) you are considering, review which cities they represent by going back to the City Cost-of-Living table in the Resources section of this book and reviewing the cities in your specific segment(s). Note each of the cities that meets your bracket value(s). For now, do not eliminate any specific city due to assumptions or preconceived notions you may have about it. They may be false assumptions! You'll have plenty of opportunities to remove cities from your list as you continue with the steps of PPRF.

Note: If you are interested in viewing the full list of curated cities, visit www.retirocracy.com/pprf/tools for more information.

At this point in using the PPRF, you should have a list of **15-125 cities** ranked by their cost-of-living value. This list represents the top cities identified by the PPRF as *most likely to meet your specific cost-of-living objectives* given your expected retirement income and your dream retirement vision. At this point you have not filtered your city results any further. Additional filtering criteria based on your personal preferences and requirements are next.

#5 Cities That Meet Persona Criteria

Your list of cities may be quite long right now, so it's time to begin eliminating some from your list. You will do that based on the most critical needs of your **Relocation Persona**. You may not have decided on your retirement persona, and now is the time to do so. Here is the list of core personas we discussed in Chapter 6:

a) Adventure
b) Affluence
c) Digital nomad
d) Return to roots
e) Better quality of life
f) Better standard of living
g) Early retirement
h) Health and wellness
i) Investment

The Retirocracy team has already researched each target city and classified each one as belonging to one or more of the above personas. Some cities may have a stronger relevance for a given persona than another city, but if the city met our minimum standard, we captured it. Some cities are good destinations for a number of personas, and you will see that, too. Just go to www.retirocracy.com/pprf/tools on the website to review our Persona Guide.

Identify the retirement persona most important to you. If you have multiple personas, be sure to select the **most critical one** at this time. If none of the personas are relevant, feel free to skip this step and proceed with the next section.

Example:

Let's assume that you select **Early Retirement** as your top persona. Go to the Persona by City guide found on the Retirocracy website, and under the "Early Retirement" section flag every city in your original list from Step #4, based on cost of living, that is associated with your selected persona.

As you do this, your initial list of cities shrinks automatically for you. After completing this step, you will have identified the cities that may meet your:

a) Dream retirement vision
b) Realistic retirement budget
c) Top persona criteria

Again, keep the evolving, filtered list that the PPRF has given you.

#6 Cities That Meet Lifestyle and Quality-of-Life Preferences

With this step, you further filter out cities and reduce the number of options to include only those which *most closely match your lifestyle and quality-of-life criteria.*

Remember that our big thrust is to create a quality life for ourselves in retirement, perhaps even a higher quality than we have in our active years. That means that you can choose what that great life looks like. You get to decide based on your dream. It also means that you will need to further fine-tune your city selections to account for those additional factors.

For instance, if a great lifestyle includes a mountainous view out of the window, Los Angeles is not for you when you retire! Remember my friends who moved from Santa Barbara to rural Arkansas (because they sought a country life), or think about someone who decided to retire to his hometown of Santa Fe (smaller town and better air quality; a hometown feeling) from Los Angeles? Those retirees sought a certain climate or terrain type, required amenities and so on.

This part of the PPRF helps you do that, too, right now. The lifestyle and quality-of-life preferences you can indicate to filter your destination cities may include:

- Weather/climate
- Topography preferences
    - Beach
    - Mountains
    - Metro area
- Distance from your "home" city
- Presence of an American or English-speaking expatriate community, if you are considering international locations
- Safety; low crime rates
- Health and wellness resources and specialties
- Luxury and shopping amenities
- Adventure/outdoors

As in the prior step, go to the Retirocracy website again to review our Lifestyle and Quality of Life guide. Be sure to flag those cities on your current list that are associated with your lifestyle and quality-of-life criteria found in our guide. And again, your list of cities will shrink.

Once you have filtered your list by lifestyle and quality of life, you should have a much more manageable list of cities to review and research. If your list still has too many cities, now is a good time to remove additional cities that you know will not meet your personal criteria.

Once you have reduced your list to less than 10 cities, you are ready to begin the next stage, which involves researching each of your cities to determine if it might fit your needs.

#7 Simple Research of Your Top Cities

Your criteria and previous filtering should leave you at this point with no more than your top 3-10 cities. Now it's time to perform a deeper analysis of the list of remaining cities. Your goal is to fine-tune for potential fit and to validate a few important assumptions you've made.

To achieve this, you'll need to ask several questions about each city on your short list. Some questions will not apply to you and you can pass (e.g., job market – that may not interest you if you won't be working). Here are some of the questions:

- Do you know anyone who lives in that city? Check your social networks.
- What are the good/bad neighborhoods?
- What's the state of the job market and entrepreneurial opportunities?
- Public transportation? Would you need to own a vehicle?
- What is the crime rate?
- Weather/climate? Is it what you want year-round or only seasonally?
- What are the amenities and services of the city/community?

- What is the general vibe of the city and its people?
- Activities, events, nightlife?
- City reviews by residents and visitors?
- Healthcare infrastructure?
- How long would it take to fly or drive back to your current city?
- Visit housing websites to learn local housing costs (rent/buy in the city).
- Tax regulations that concern you?
- Any government approvals/authorizations (e.g.: residency visa)?

Go to www.retirocracy.com/pprf/tools and download our "Research Questions" guide for the complete list of research questions to consider for your list of top cities.

At this point you'll need to rely on your own instincts and judgment to determine which cities are still under consideration, based on your researched responses to our selected questions. While there's always the possibility that all of your short-listed cities remain on your list, or all of the remaining cities are removed from your list, in most cases you should have a small number of remaining cities to consider.

It's also important to keep in mind that much like your current city of residence, other cities also have many distinct neighborhoods and communities. For example, this means that just because a destination city on your list might have both good and bad neighborhoods (and don't they all?), doesn't mean you should cross that city off your short list. It just means you now know where you will not look for housing if you were to move there! If the city has lots of nightlife, that likewise is not a reason to cross it off if you are an early-to-bed person. Bottom line: Use your judgment!

I'd suggest at this point simply taking notes on the answers you get. Then, with your notes and short list of cities in hand, move to the next step for more in-depth research.

#8 Extensively Research Your Top Cities

Up to this point you have been filtering cities to get matches on your criteria and preferences. Now I recommend that you search and target more general types of information to round out the informational picture about each city on your short list. Use online sources such as the following as your starting point.

Google: Just typing in the city name (and nothing more at first) can yield an overwhelming number of sites ready to answer your most specific or general questions. Look at the more serious ones rather than blogs/vlogs/articles at this point. Look at the city's history, economics, educational offerings and levels, its political organization, transportation, shopping and (this is my favorite question) … find out what its claim to fame is! Is it a modern, international city? Is it known for its centuries-old university? Is it the home of a famous citizen, sports team or culinary school? Find out all you can. It will situate the city in your mind in relation to the others.

.Org and .Gov: I find that the dot-org or dot-gov (.org; .gov) sites are serious information providers. The dot-gov city-related sites will naturally be favorably biased as they are representing their cities to the world, so keep that in mind; they often have sections on moving to or living in the city, and often that information cannot be found elsewhere. Dot-org sites are generally reserved for non-profit or foundation sites. If they have a connection to your destination city, find out what it is. (It might also show places you can volunteer.)

- www.usa.gov/local-governments
- nextcity.org/

Blogs: Remember that blogs are written by individuals, not organizations. Tens of thousands of locally focused blogs exist, and those individuals writing them are quite often (but not always) skilled, knowledgeable, passionate writers on aspects of your target cities. Just read them with the proverbial "grain of salt."

- www.google.com : Enter in search box "blogs about _(city name)"
- www.fwweekly.com/blogs/

- www.gringoinbuenosaires.com/blog/
- www.paperplanesblog.com/

Vlogs: These are video-oriented blogs, so expect to see similar information found on blogs in a more visual format. Like blogs, vlogs are typically created by individuals, not organizations, and include varying degrees of accuracy and relevance, so keep that in mind as you view them. On the Google results page, click the "Video" menu items to sort for only the latest videos about the city. Search YouTube for videos by actual travelers to the city, as well as videos produced by residents.

- www.google.com: Enter in search box "videos about _*(city name)*"
- Enter your target city on www.youtube.com

Videos by organizations: Search YouTube for "documentaries about _(your destination city/country)." These are often better researched (and filmed) than individual vlogs. Look for them by producers such as …

- National Geographic
- BBC productions
- Short travel/location-specific documentaries

City articles/news: Note that articles may be blogs or articles by news media or by organizations such as universities or businesses. Google "articles about _(city name)" and see what results you get. On the Google results page, click the "News" menu item to sort for only the latest or most-read past news about the city or businesses and the people of the city.

- www.southeasterntraveler.com/blog/2015/01/6-things-i-love-about-knoxville-tennessee/
- https://www.papernstitchblog.com/2016/05/05/scottsdale-arizona-travel-guide/
- https://www.nomadasaurus.com/3-days-in-buenos-aires/

Online City Newspapers: Google "_(city name) newspapers."

- https://www.syracusenewtimes.com/
- http://www.vvdailypress.com/desert-dispatch
- https://www.ambergristoday.com/

Social media: Look for city-focused network groups and forums.

  - Look for "_(city name) groups" on Facebook. For example, Facebook has a Santa Fe Bulletin Board Public Group. Ask your active social media friends if they have firsthand knowledge about any of your destination cities, then ask them for advice, tips, information, other websites or books they know of.

- Twitter has, for instance, a City of Santa Clara Group and The Santa Fe Group, and that means you can locate the accounts of your destination cities and follow them.

Bottom line, be creative in your research strategies for learning more about each city on your list. The internet has made it significantly easier to discover, learn and validate our understanding of any city around the globe, so take advantage.

#9 Tour Your Short-Listed Cities

Deciding to relocate to a new city should not be taken lightly. This is where the rubber meets the road. You put on your walking shoes, grab your travel bag and go see each of the short-listed cities with your own eyes. This is how you compare your remote research results with the realities on the ground – in fact, it is the only way to do it right.

Determine the best time of year (or specific month) to visit. Are there annual events, such as carnivals or street fairs, that offer a better sense of the community and local experience? When and where are the farmers' markets, car shows, community events, concerts and volunteer opportunities?

Get out of the hotel as much as possible and spend a few days exploring and immersing yourself in the culture and lifestyle. As part of your tour, branch out and include activities that might not have interested you in the past:

- Arts and culture (museums, live concerts, ballet, theatrical performances).
- Architecture and history (guided walking or bus tours with a historian).
- Transportation (test the bus or subway system on your own; find out how to buy tickets and pre-pay monthly tickets and options for your age group or demographic).
- Dining and nightlife (culinary options and prices; go out for a drink at a club, even if you normally wouldn't – and chat with people for an hour).
- Amenities (hospitals, community night courses, sports-for-seniors centers or activities, clubs for your hobbies, free outdoor events).
- Commerce (types of shopping – malls, boutiques, open-air or farmers' markets).
- Housing (visit rental/for sale homes and apartments, both new constructions and renovations, in all the parts of town you have earmarked).

Get outside the city, too, and into the countryside. Are there places to visit, relax, eat different foods, and discover new cultural or leisure interests? Your trip should be well-planned, and include a blend of on-your-own and formal tours of the city and surrounding areas of interest.

Remember: The top goal of your trip is to validate or invalidate your assumptions and expectations about the city.

Note: You'll find a template on Retirocracy.com that provides a detailed framework for visiting and rating any city you visit.

#10 Engage With the Local Community and Local Experts

Touring a city firsthand is an important activity for validating a city. Spending time with locals is just as important. As part of your city tour, make it a point to identify people in advance who you can meet with to gain an insider's understanding of life in that city.

Try to connect with a recent relocator (American, or anyone who you share a common language with if you will travel abroad), ideally someone who has lived in the city for less than five years. You want to chat with those who can offer an insightful perspective on pros and cons of the city, and point you to various attractions, activities, clubs and events to experience while you are in town.

An attorney is your next consultation, to explain any legal considerations about relocating. If you plan to work there, will your current certifications or licenses be valid? If the city is not in the U.S., will you need a visa and how will a desire to work affect the type of visa you request? What about banking? How do you maximize your income, while minimizing any tax liabilities associated with living in the new city?

Talk to a banker or two in the major banks (or the local branch of your current bank), to establish new banking relationships. Meeting with a banker from a reputable bank is a good way to ground yourself in a stable, reputable network of financial professionals.

Realtors are there to guide you through the available housing, costs and formalities, as well as set up visits, whether you are buying or renting. Spend time not only touring neighborhoods on foot but entering available residences with a realtor. Be sure to visit communities similar to your current one and some that are very different; get a feel for the city that way. The point is to never limit your options when seeking to get a complete understanding of the housing options available to you. A good realtor can help you plan a thoughtful and extensive housing tour.

#11 Take Another, Extended Trip

After you have returned home and fully digested the experience of your first trip to the destination city, you should have a clear idea of whether the city meets your expectations and requirements. If it doesn't, there are other cities on your list. If you are satisfied with what you've experienced in the city, then I'd strongly recommend that you take **a second trip** to the city, this time for an extended period, say, three to six weeks.

This is an important step because visiting a new community for less than three weeks doesn't always provide a full picture of the experience. The novelty of a new city can sometimes take two weeks or more to wear off.

On this second trip, plan and schedule your activities similar to the prior trip. However, this time it will be important to allocate pockets of ad hoc time when you will just casually explore the city. It's important not to rush; you can absorb the beauty and the differences of the city at a slower and more comfortable pace. Do most things without a formal guide this time to get a good feel for how they unfold for you. You are likely to observe things, both good and bad, that you missed on the first trip.

Spend more time casually making local acquaintances and connections. Ask locals what they like and dislike about their city. Ask what they do to earn their livings. Check in again with your previous professional contacts for more discussions on the real estate, banking, financial or legal aspects of living here.

Above all, do things that help you understand fully what the real cost of living and your real purchase power is in this city. Cook some meals for yourself after shopping in the markets, if that is how you feed yourself (or go to restaurants if that is your retirement habit) and keep receipts of everything you buy. Compare the costs of here and back home. Are the expected lower costs a reality in this new city? Keep some notes about that.

#12 Finalize Your Decision

Congrats for making it to this point. You need to make a decision! You have a short list of one to three cities. You've done online research, taken personal trips to the city, you have met some of the residents and professionals.

By the way, a few people I have spoken to about "just moving" for retirement did not do this depth of research for moves to cities they ended up living and working in for over 15 years! You are way ahead of the game.

Now make a list of pros and cons and consider your top priorities. Is it important to be near your family? Is it important to walk to the beach? Do you want to live in a climate of never-changing 75-degree weather? Are cycling or deep-sea fishing important to you?

Once you make your core list of top requirements and really think about what your needs are, it'll be much easier to make the final decision. At the end of the day, it is all about your happiness. It's okay to make certain sacrifices to be happy, just make sure you are making the right sacrifices. If you keep an open mind, consider the pros and cons and weigh your priorities, it will lead to a much happier and fulfilling retirement experience.

Certainly, continue to do more homework on this location. Now that you have chosen one city, your mind will churn with new questions. Go online and Google things. Skype or Facebook some of the people you met there and ask your questions. Be respectful of their time, remembering they won't have all the answers (only those they know from personal experience).

#13 Prepare for Transition and Moving

You've selected your destination. You've hopefully visited it a few times and seen your increased purchase power firsthand. You've collected lots of information and met a good number of new people.

Now you move! Yes, depending on where you move to, it may resemble every other move you've made in your life. Here are a few tips to make the experience as smooth and seamless as possible:

- Find a reputable realtor and start visiting, costing and choosing local housing right away. Remember that housing is likely to be your greatest expense, so spend the time early on to select a home that maximizes cost and value.
- Confirm and secure that housing choice as soon as you can (rent and deposits; purchase).
- Wander around your new neighborhood and town center, and "feel its heartbeat."

- Figure out where the best local shops and businesses are for your needs and wants and budget.
- Sign up for local language classes (if applicable) or organize your own tutor in your new home – consider university students, other local retirees or professional teachers as great tutors.
- Seek out groups and events that would allow you to begin engaging with the community and your surroundings. Think about hiking clubs, hobby clubs, volunteer organizations looking for helping hands like yours, etc.
- Get a mobile phone with a local number, especially important for overseas relocations. Make sure local friends have it; give it to people back home.
- Ask select friends and/or family to confirm a trip to visit you in your new location. Help them prepare and be excited about it.
- Become part of the community, and someone with things to do and people to see! Do not wait for a week or a month to get involved – jump right in during the first three to four days after you've moved in. Get involved with your new community immediately!
- Be prepared to develop a new routine. You may eat breakfast earlier or later than before and enjoy different foods. You may stay out later than you were used to in pre-retirement days, due to the pace of local life or its cultural offerings. You may find you are walking more than ever – and loving

it. Or volunteering, when you never did that before. Remain open to the newness and to some change!

- Give yourself permission to feel homesick. Give yourself permission to NOT understand everything and everyone right away! Let the feelings pass … they do.
- Be grateful for everything.
- Be friendly and polite to everyone.

There is no doubt in my mind that my own retirement years hold much adventure in store for me. Why should we think our retirement will be just more of the same? I'm excited and optimistic, not fearful.

Sure, there might be a surprise or two along the way, but by planning with our Purchase Power Retirement Formula, you can have confidence that not meeting your retirement savings goal will not have undue influence on whether your dream retirement is achievable or not.

Prepare more fully on all fronts. Planning with the PPRF will take away a massive amount of the stress inherent in any move you might make.

My retirement will not be just more of the same, because that is not how I am envisaging and planning it. You can dream it and see it and create it any way you like. Your retirement can be more of the same, of course, if that is your choice. You can also experience a brand-new world to its fullest while writing the next chapter of your life.

The Retirocracy.com website is your first stop, as it makes implementing PPRF simple and easy – so please go to the site and perform the entire PPRF for yourself. The Retirocracy support team is a resource available to you to make the stages of your discovery, evaluation, planning and relocation easy and painless. My team and I have made additional materials and content available to you, via the Retirocracy website, to simplify applying the PPRF system. If interested, we are also available for direct consultations to help guide you through your relocation journey.

We can provide more specific tools that can simplify your discovery and research of various cities. When you and our team members chat, we can connect you with local hosts in each of your short-listed destination cities to help you discover those cities most effectively.

One thing I learned when I lost all my retirement wealth during the financial and mortgage crash of 2007-08: It is never too late to save more, to plan for a great retirement, to dream and to take actions to materialize the dream. Get going now. The Purchase Power Retirement Formula is helping lots of people every year to let go of the #1 retirement worry: "Can we ever afford to retire and experience the retirement we deserve?" The PPRF proves that we all can!

Remember the Retirement Manifesto that Retirocracy operates by? It is now possible for you to rewrite it to suit your own goals and lifestyle choices. The Manifesto declares that you plan to live your retirement years – at whatever age they start and however long they last – your way.

CONCLUSION:

YOUR INVITATION

So that's the Purchase Power Retirement Formula. You may be feeling a bit overwhelmed, or you may be feeling a rush of excitement. Either way, you can move forward with the confidence in knowing that millions of people have successfully relocated based on the core principles that PPRF are based on. You can also find confidence in knowing that countless retirees have successfully relocated locally, regionally, across the U.S. and internationally. My hope is that instead of feeling frustrated or overwhelmed, you'll feel empowered after realizing that PPRF provides you with a huge shortcut in achieving your own goals.

If you're wondering where you should start, I'd suggest:

1. Set a clear vision: Become VERY clear about what your dream retirement would look like, regardless of your budget.
2. Be honest: Given your current savings trajectory, admit what your financial gap or deficit is likely to be when you retire.
3. Be curious: Discover and explore the various cities in the U.S. and abroad. Learn which locations resonate with you and why. Always be mindful of the cost of living and purchase power factor of your city vs. any other.
4. Avoid the status quo: Following everyone else, in this regard, may lead to an inferior outcome. With age comes less risk-taking and more rigidity. Don't allow any of these habits to undermine your ability to make the best changes for you and experience YOUR dream retirement, wherever it may be.

I hope that reading this book has helped you refine your vision. I spent several years researching and over a year writing and rewriting it in hopes that it would educate, inspire and excite you. But understand that reading the book is only the first step. The book will never be as good as using my online support tools and resources at www.retirocracy.com, or having me or my team work with you personally to identify the best cities for you and helping you tour those top locations and their respective communities. If you'd like help or support in taking the next step to plan your dream retirement, I invite you to visit our site, watch our Video Series, and/or attend one of our many Dream Retirement Webinar events.

The Video Series will provide you with a different view into some of the information discussed in the book. The videos will help reinforce several of the core concepts discussed here and offer personal stories from real people who have benefited from the principles PPRF are based on.

During the Dream Retirement Webinar, we spend time with a small group of people discussing the details of PPRF, invite special guests to share their real stories, and provide you an opportunity to ask questions. If you would be interested in either offering, visit www.retirocracy.com for more information.

I also invite you to join our private Facebook group of like-minded people, eager to experience the retirement they deserve.

Now it's your turn to take the next step. Whether you decide to embrace relocation or another strategy for achieving your retirement goals, I hope that after reading Part 1, you better understand the challenges that await you and the pending retirement crisis that has slowly unfolded over the past decade or more. For those who are unprepared or not on track for retirement, don't expect your government or anyone else to magically save you. If history is a guide, you'll need to rely on and trust yourself. Bottom line: Now is the time to define and put your plan into action if you haven't already.

Regardless of what you determine as the best retirement strategy for you, if after reading this book you have a heightened urgency to do something and you are less inclined to wait for the retirement funding system to fix itself, then I've succeeded. Now if you ask me for my opinion on what to do next, I am, of course, a passionate advocate for adopting a relocation strategy to meet your desired retirement goals. The benefits are plenty and the risks are minimal. But ultimately that's your decision.

I've personally observed countless people relocate successfully for a variety of reasons. Whether it was to retire early, for adventure, a better quality of life, investment, lower cost of living, lifestyle upgrade, or any other reason – I've seen it all. But I've also seen the consequences of relocating without a sound approach.

It's easy to understand why people make mistakes when seeking to relocate. Relocating for retirement seems simple. You just pick a location that "appears" to be a good fit for personal reasons, maybe you know people who live there, maybe you read a glowing article on the city in a popular magazine, or perhaps you visited the city during a vacation and fell in love with the lifestyle. In any case, you found your little slice of paradise and now you are ready to move. In reality, however, there are many reasons that can make a seemingly dream city an actual nightmare. To start, you might discover after living there that it does not meet your financial, social, cultural and/or lifestyle needs. So, to minimize any chance of failure, you need a pragmatic approach that will help you surface all of your top needs, identify cities that may meet those needs, and help you effectively validate your options.

It's Your Move

Now the next step is up to you. My primary goal for this book was to show you the opportunity that relocation offers as part of your broader retirement strategy. The secondary goal was to share, via PPRF, a disciplined, proven process for minimizing risk and maximizing success in relocating.

By now the opportunity should be clear. A relocation strategy is one of the few retirement strategies that doesn't require you to make or save more money to be successful. Instead this approach helps you magnify and maximize your expected savings and income, whatever it might be, by identifying cities that offer you enough leverage and cost savings to make up whatever your savings gap might be.

Now that doesn't mean you should stop implementing strategies that focus on making more money, saving more money or investing better. Those approaches are critical to your success and should never stop. However, it does mean that you need a solid "fallback" plan. So regardless of where you land in your retirement-savings goal, you will have the peace of mind in knowing you can still achieve a first-class retirement experience.

The key is to take action early and often, or more specifically, to take that first step and then several smaller steps afterward. Don't expect to discover the perfect city after a few hours of applying the formula. Expect it to take more time to find the right city than you anticipated. Expect frustrations and head-scratching; it's part of the journey! Most importantly, expect to be enlightened and surprised by what you learn and discover from this experience. Expect to be empowered by the new opportunities and practical solutions that help you successfully achieve YOUR dream retirement.

The Journey Continues

What a ride it has been so far. I could've never imagined that my desire to retire by 40 with my first million would have ever led to helping others discover relocation as a pivotal strategy for their retirement.

There are countless articles released daily reiterating the looming retirement crisis and lack of viable solutions. If you tune into the news regularly, you know exactly what I'm referring to. I want future retirees to know that there are retirement solutions that will empower them to successfully retire, or as I like to say, achieve their dream retirement. My goal is to continue sharing the benefits of PPRF with as many people as possible.

PPRF will work for you. Just follow the steps I shared in this book. To make your process better, faster and easier, leverage the additional tools and resources we've made available to you on Retirocracy.com.

Finally, nothing energizes me more than hearing people successfully relocate for retirement, or helping others discover a city that enables them to achieve their best retirement. If you have relocated somewhere as part of your retirement strategy and have a story to share, I would love to hear from you. If you haven't moved anywhere else, but are considering relocation, I would love to hear from you as well. Email me and let me know your experience or story. Hearing your stories is the best part of this experience for me. You can reach me at idris.pprf@retirocracy.com.

All the best in your pursuit of a phenomenal retirement experience.

Resources

Website: www.retirocracy.com

Your PPRF tools for this book: www.retirocracy.com/pprf/tools

Facebook: www.facebook.com/retirocracy

Instagram: www.instagram.com/retirocracy

YouTube: www.youtube.com/retirocracy

Twitter: https://twitter.com/retirocracy

Cost-of-Living Table:

Domestic City	State	Level
Los Angeles	California	5
Chicago	Illinois	7
Houston	Texas	7
Phoenix	Arizona	7
Philadelphia	Pennsylvania	7
San Antonio	Texas	7
San Diego	California	5
Dallas	Texas	7
San Jose	California	3
Austin	Texas	6

Jacksonville	Florida	7
San Francisco	California	1
Columbus	Ohio	7
Indianapolis	Indiana	7
Fort Worth	Texas	7
Charlotte	North Carolina	7
Seattle	Washington	4
Denver	Colorado	6
El Paso	Texas	8
Washington	District of Columbia	5
Boston	Massachusetts	4
Detroit	Michigan	8
Nashville[14]	Tennessee	7

International City	**Country**	**Level**
Santiago	Chile	8
Medellin	Colombia	9
San Jose	Costa Rica	8
Santo Domingo	Dominican Republic	8
Cuenca	Ecuador	8
Paris	France	6
Bali	Indonesia	8
Bologna	Italy	7
Rome	Italy	7
Kingston	Jamaica	7
Nairobi	Kenya	8
Kuala Lumpur	Malaysia	8
Sliema	Malta	7
Cancun	Mexico	9

Guadalajara	Mexico	9
Lagos	Nigeria	9
Panama City	Panama	8
Manila	Philippines	9
Quezon City	Philippines	9
Valenzuela	Philippines	9
Lisbon	Portugal	8
Algarve	Portugal	10
Cape Town	South Africa	8
Barcelona	Spain	7
Chiang Mai	Thailand	8
Montevideo	Uruguay	7
Hanoi	Vietnam	8

Check out our Video Series, which expands on the PPRF concepts discussed in the book and offers additional insights into successfully adopting PPRF for retirement. For more information, visit www.retirocracy.com/pprf/video-series

End Notes

1 https://www.nationwide.com/personal/about-us/newsroom/press-release?title=091917-nf-social-security

2 https://www.ml.com/articles/age-wave-survey.html

3 https://ourworldindata.org/life-expectancy; https://www.theatlantic.com/business/archive/2014/10/how-retirement-was-invented/381802/

4 https://www.epi.org/resources/research_data/

5 https://www.cnbc.com/2017/06/13/heres-how-many-americans-have-nothing-at-all-saved-for-retirement.html

6 https://www.forbes.com/sites/kateashford/2018/02/28/retirement-3/

7 Compensation research firm, *Payscale*

8 *Age Disparities in Unemployment and Reemployment during the Great Recession and Recovery*, by Richard W. Johnson and Barbara A. Butrica

9 https://smartasset.com/credit-cards/the-average-debt-by-age

10 https://www.ssa.gov/history/briefhistory3.html

11 https://www.thebalance.com/the-history-of-the-pension-plan-2894374

12 https://www.cnbc.com/2017/01/04/a-brief-history-of-the-401k-which-changed-how-americans-retire.html

13 Federal Reserve's *2016 Survey of Consumer Finances* - https://www.federalreserve.gov/econres/scfindex.htm

14 https://www.fidelity.com/viewpoints/personal-finance/plan-for-rising-health-care-costs; Fidelity Investments

15 https://www.thestreet.com/retirement/18-facts-about-womens-retirement-14558073; Center for Retirement Research at Boston College - http://crr.bc.edu/; GAO (Government Accountability Office) - https://www.gao.gov/

16 https://www.cheatsheet.com/money-career/surprising-american-savings-statistics.html/?a=viewall; https://www.cnbc.com/2017/09/13/how-much-americans-at-have-in-their-savings-accounts.html; https://www.theatlantic.com/business/archive/2018/02/pensions-safety-net-california/553970/

17 Mortgage Bankers Association Special Report by Gary V. Engelhardt – Housing Trends Among Baby Boomers; U.S. Census Bureau's 2016 Current Population Survey Annual Social and Economic Supplement (CPS ASEC) - https://www.census.gov/newsroom/blogs/random-samplings/2017/01/mover-rate.html

18 http://www.mybudget360.com/cost-of-living-1975-and-2017-inflation-purchasing-power-dollar/

19 *The State of Opportunity in America Report;* Gallup survey co-published with the Center for Advancing Opportunity

20 https://www.census.gov/data/tables/2017/demo/geographic-mobility/cps-2017.html

21 Bad Money – The Inexcusable Failure of American Finance: An Update to Bad Money, and Bad Money – Reckless Finance, Failed Politics, and the Global Crisis of American Capitalism, books authored by political commentator Kevin Phillips –https://www.amazon.com/Bad-Money-Inexcusable-American-eSpecial/dp/0143114808

22 Survey by the international money transfer company *TransferWise* - https://transferwise.com/us/blog/americans-ready-to-move-abroad

23 https://livability.com/topics/moving/why-do-peo-

ple-move-here-are-the-top-reasons-for-relocation
https://www.state.gov/r/pa/ei/bgn/35749.htm

24 https://www.quora.com/Why-would-an-American-want-to-retire-in-a-developing-country